IF IT FEELS GOOD

Also by Joan Elizabeth Lloyd

NICE COUPLES DO

IF IT FEELS GOOD

Using the Five Senses to Enhance Your Lovemaking

Joan Elizabeth Lloyd

WARNER BOOKS

A Time Warner Company

Copyright © 1993 by Joan Elizabeth Lloyd
All rights reserved.

Warner Books, Inc., 1271 Avenue of the Americas, New York, NY 10020

W A Time Warner Company

Printed in the United States of America
First printing: January 1993

ISBN 0-446-39450-5

Cover photograph by Barnaby Hall
Cover design by Diane Luger
Book design by Giorgetta Bell McRee

*This book is dedicated to Ed,
with whom, through love, trust, and communication,
all things are possible.*

CONTENTS

CONTENTS

"Doctor," Betty said, "I need some advice. Jack and I have been married for four years and I love him very much. But he wants to make love all the time. Not just every night but often in the morning or at lunchtime. Our love life is wonderful, but I'm exhausted."

"But, dear," her husband said, "the sight of your lovely body, the smell of your perfume, the taste of your lips, and the feel of your skin drive me wild. I want you all the time."

The counselor thought a while, then said, "Timing is frequently a problem in sexual relationships and usually calls for compromise. Why don't you try this. Jack," he said to the husband, "I want you to try having sex with Betty only on days with the letter n in them. That limits you to Sunday, Monday, Wednesday. Betty, you try to get some rest on the other days."

"Okay," the couple said in unison. "We'll try."

"Come back in a few weeks and we'll see how everything worked out."

On the first morning of the following weekend, Jack woke up early. He was immediately aware of Betty's body next to him in bed. The sight of her beautiful breasts, the sound of her soft breathing, the special smell of her body all conspired to make him regret his promise. Slowly, he snuggled up to his wife and nudged her awake.

"Betty, darling," he purred, "happy Snaturday."

IF IT FEELS GOOD

1

IF IT GIVES YOU PLEASURE...

CAROL AND TIM'S STORY

"**H**appy fifth anniversary, sweetheart," Carol said.

"Don't be silly," her husband, Tim, said, settling on the sofa. "I was wondering why you cooked that special dinner, and I don't object, mind you, but our fifth anniversary isn't until next April."

"Not the anniversary of our wedding," Carol said, a glint in her eye. "Exactly five years ago today, we made love for the first time."

Tim thought a moment. "You know, you're right." He smiled at her. "I should have realized that you would remember that kind of thing. You're such a romantic."

Carol pulled a package wrapped in silver foil from beside the sofa. From the shape, it obviously contained a wine bottle. "This is for you."

"Obviously, I didn't get anything for you," Tim said.

He untied the red ribbon from around the neck of the bottle and pulled it out. When he saw the label, he laughed out loud. "This is the same awful red wine we had that night. It tasted slightly like tree bark." Tim unscrewed the cap and inhaled. "And it smelled like it, too."

"I know," Carol said, handing him two glasses. "But I thought we should have some for old times' sake."

"I think that's a great idea." Tim poured two glasses of wine while Carol put a tape in the cassette player. As the strains of Glen Miller filled the room, Tim took a sip of the wine. "This is as terrible as I remember it being, but it does bring back some wonderful memories." He listened to the music for a minute. "So does that music. I think that was the first thing I liked about you. You shared my love of the big bands." He paused, then said, "We played Glen Miller that night, didn't we?"

"Sure did. I remember that evening so well. The taste of that wine, the sound of that tape."

Tim thought back. "Do you remember that terrible vanilla-scented candle we lighted?"

With a grin, Carol pulled out another foil-wrapped package, this one a small box.

"You didn't," Tim said as he removed the wrapping. He opened the box inside and withdrew a candle. "You're amazing."

Carol went into the kitchen and rummaged around in a drawer until she found a match. She placed the short, fat candle on a plate, lighted it, and placed it on the coffee table in front of Tim. After a moment, the room was filled with the familiar aroma.

"You know," Carol said, "it still smells like I just baked a batch of sugar cookies, but it brings back such wonderful times."

In silence, they sipped their wine. Then Carol turned to Tim. "You know what I would like?" she asked.

"What?"

"I would like to make love with you right here on the sofa like we did that night." She wrapped her arms around Tim's neck and kissed him softly. "Do you remember? We kissed until we thought we'd go crazy from wanting."

They kissed, Tim's hands softly stroking Carol's back. When they parted, Tim said, "I also remember how hesitant and passive you were. That's the only thing I would change."

"I know," Carol said, kissing him again on the mouth. "I've read the articles you bookmarked for me and I've heard the stories you tell me while we make love. That's why I bought all this stuff." Carol had known for a while that Tim wanted her to be more aggressive. He had slipped bookmarks into several stories about women who initiated sex with their partner. "I want to take a more active role in our lovemaking. It's just awkward for me. But I'm learning. Tonight, I wanted to be the one to light the candles."

"God, I love you." Tim pressed his wife back until she was stretched out on the sofa. "I remember the first time I touched you." He reached up under Carol's sweater and touched her breasts through her bra. "It was a few weeks before we first made love." He fondled her dreamily. "You were so soft that I thought I'd died and gone to heaven."

Tim deftly slipped his hand behind Carol and unsnapped her bra. He grinned. "I still haven't lost my touch." He pulled her bra up under her sweater and swirled his fingers around the soft, warm flesh of her breast. "And you still feel wonderful."

"Ummm," Carol purred into his ear. "And you feel even better now than you did then." She pulled his shirttails out and used them to pull him closer so she could whisper into his ear. "As you know, you weren't the first to touch my breasts, but what you may not know is that you were the first one who ever saw all of me naked."

She slipped from his grasp and quickly pulled off her clothes. She stood beside the couch and watched Tim's eyes roam over her body. Mingled with the knowledge that she was making love to her husband was the feeling that a young, virginal girl was letting a man look at her body for the first time.

When Tim had looked his fill, he stood up to undress, but Carol captured his hands and held them at his sides. "Let this be just a bit different from that night." She pulled his belt from the buckle and opened the front of his jeans. "Let me do this." Slowly, she peeled his jeans down over his hips. She could see the outline of his erection through his underpants. "You were the first man I saw completely naked, too."

Quickly, she removed his shirt and pulled off his undershirt, her feelings a mixture of her newfound aggressiveness and the memory of the wonder of their first time. She bent down and lifted each foot and pulled off his shoes and socks.

She stood, and as she kissed her husband, she

pressed the length of her body against him. Provocatively, she pressed her pelvis against his erection, still sheathed in his shorts. "So good, darling," she said. "So good."

Tim was in heaven. Never before had his wife behaved this way. He didn't want to move for fear she would spook.

Carol stepped away and slipped her fingers under the waistband of his shorts. Agonizingly slowly, she pulled the shorts down, allowing his hard erection to spring from his underpants.

"You have no idea how much I want you," he groaned.

Carol placed a tiny kiss on the tip of his penis. "I have some idea."

Tim was beyond much control. "I know it's very fast, but I want to make love to you right now. I feel the same urgency I felt that night."

"There's one more present."

Tim groaned as Carol handed him a small package. He didn't want to wait. He wanted to toss her down on the sofa and fuck her brains out. Patiently, however, he tore off the wrappings and inside was a package of condoms, exactly the same brand he had used that night. "I don't believe it. They're the same kind. But we don't need these now; you're on the pill."

"I know that," Carol said, "but I want as many of the same sensations we shared that night as possible." She pushed Tim back onto the sofa as she gently took the package from him. "Let me."

Tim was flabbergasted. As they made love, he had

whispered stories in her ear about women who occasionally took the lead in bed, but never before had Carol actually seemed to get the message. Now he watched as she placed the latex condom on the end of his penis.

Carol wasn't sure she knew how to put the condom on, but she found that it was easy. She unrolled the latex as she pushed it down over Tim's increasingly hard penis. She smiled as she inhaled the slightly plastic smell and remembered that night five years before. She had smelled that smell then and she had known what Tim was doing. They hadn't discussed protection, but she recalled how glad she had been that he was so responsible. As she remembered how hungry she had been then, she was amazed at how wet and hungry she was now.

As Tim reached down to touch her, she pushed his hands away. She wanted this evening to go her way. She was surprised at how much she was enjoying being the leader.

When the condom was completely in place, Carol stood up beside the couch. She knew Tim wanted her and she wanted him, as well. But she didn't want to be touched; she didn't want anything except the feel of him inside of her. She looked down at her husband lying on the sofa and knew exactly how she desired him. She lifted one leg, straddled him, and, with one knee on the sofa and one foot still on the floor, she impaled herself on his cock.

"Oh God," Tim cried as he felt her tighten her vaginal muscles around him. "If you do that, you're going to make me come."

"That's exactly what I had in mind," Carol said, her voice low and breathy. "Come inside me." She lifted her hips and again slammed herself down on his cock. "Come because I want you to. Now."

Between the sight and feel of his wife's body and the sound of her words, he climaxed, screaming, "Oh God, yes. Yes."

Carol was completely happy. It didn't seem to matter that she hadn't had an orgasm. The feel of her husband's hips bucking against her and his penis pulsing deep inside her gave her all the pleasure she could stand. She collapsed on top of him.

When they had regained their composure, Tim said, "That was incredible."

"I gather you liked it."

"Liked it?" he said, laughing. "It was sensational. It was terrific when we first made love five years ago and even better tonight." Tim sighed and wrapped his arms around his wife. "You know, it's amazing how I can make love to the same woman I've been making love to for five years and it can still seem so new and exciting." He gave her a squeeze. "And later we have to talk about this new aggressive you and how we can get her to stick around. Right now, however, if it's all right with you, I'd like to adjourn to the bedroom for a short nap and a rematch."

"Sounds wonderful," Carol said. "And I have to admit that this evening was even better than five years ago."

"It certainly was."

Lovemaking is an ever-renewable pleasure. It can be as wonderful the thousandth time as it was the first. It

can take a few minutes or a few hours, or the pre-
ludes can last all day, constantly rewhetting your
appetite.

For many couples, however, instead of practice
making perfect, repetition leads to boredom. Lovemaking begins with the same signals, proceeds through
a nice but predictable period of foreplay, and ends
with intercourse in the same position they've used
since the first time they made love—comfortable but
not terrific.

Sometimes comfort and familiarity are pleasant.
More often, however, you want something more.
Maybe neither you nor your partner is sure what
"more" is. Or one or both of you may know what you
want but be unable to communicate your desires
successfully. Perhaps you believe your ideas are so
bizarre that you dare not risk mentioning them
even to your partner or you just think he wouldn't
be interested in the secret things that turn you
on.

So you go on as before, two people not quite
satisfied yet unable to talk about ways of making sex
better.

Carol and Tim had the same difficulties. Tim fantasized about women who initiated sex, who allowed
him to remain passive. At first, it was difficult for Tim
to discuss his sexual preferences with Carol, so he
tried to use body language. He dropped hints and
hoped that she would pick up on them.

Then Tim discovered bookmarking. He slipped a
bookmark in an article about a woman who was
sexually aggressive and left the magazine on Carol's

bedside table. He also began to tell stories to spice up his lovemaking with her. In those stories, the woman took an active role in the sex play. As we saw in the story, Carol eventually got the message. She also took the risk and acted out what she thought Tim had in mind.

Variety—Carol and Tim yearned for it. But, in the age of AIDS, the itch for something different can't be safely scratched at the local singles bar or with a one-night stand. And Carol and Tim didn't want different partners. They wanted to share new experiences with each other, to learn together. Now they have begun to experiment with ways to make the most of their full-time relationship, and the rewards are obvious.

Carol and Tim are learning that sex can be fun: fun to contemplate, fun to approach, fun to do.

That sex can be fun should be self-evident, but frequently it isn't. Too often sex becomes serious, even grim.

Will he climax before I do?

Will she be ready for me when I'm ready for her?

Am I wet enough yet?

Am I hard enough yet?

Will he climax?

Will I climax?

Partners are often so involved in the ending that they forget to have fun getting there.

Will he touch me here where I've always wanted him to?

Will she stroke me and squeeze me?

Will he read my body language when I try to tell him not to bite so hard?

Will she be horrified if I want to have anal sex?

Will he laugh if I want to light the candles?

Will she laugh if I put on some of the old records?

Couples often worry so much about each other's expectations that they overlook the opportunity to clarify them with a simple question or a short conversation. However, as Carol and Tim found out, if talking about intimate things is too threatening or intimidating, there are other ways to communicate.

For starters, you can use the bookmarking technique. In this book, you'll find many erotic stories. If one of these appeals to you and you can't find the words to verbalize your desire, slip a bookmark in the story, underline a passage, or dog-ear a page. Then give the book to your partner.

If you receive a bookmarked story and the section that your partner has bookmarked doesn't appeal to you, read on and move the bookmark to a section that does excite you. Then return the book. You've now begun a sexual dialogue. The beginning is always the most difficult part. It gets so much easier and so much better.

If you have something to communicate that isn't explicitly mentioned here, read a story out loud and deviate from the text to venture into the area that interests you. You can also use the story starters on pages 66–93 to create an original tale.

If you find that a part of this book doesn't interest you, skip it and go on to another section or story, although you never know what might turn you on if you give it a chance. Please, however, don't judge.

Forget the words *good* and *bad*. Use the words *fun* and *not my thing* instead.

Over the six years we've been together, my partner, Ed, and I have encountered problems, suffered embarrassments, and taken risks. We have learned so many things. We've learned to laugh; to ask, "Was that okay?"; to say, "That feels so good" and "Do that some more," especially while we are trying something new. We've learned the importance of reinforcing all the good feelings. And we've learned that making love isn't an endurance contest, so we can now freely say, "That's not wonderful" or "How about this instead." We have learned how to say no to an activity without saying or inferring that anyone was a bad person for suggesting it.

I must say something very important here. I am putting it in italics for extra emphasis. *No sexual activity that is mutually agreed upon by two adults and that gives them pleasure is bad.* Let go of all your prejudices. But also remember that everything isn't for everyone, either. There are things that I don't enjoy and things that Ed doesn't like. That's fine. Occasionally, it gives me so much pleasure to please Ed that I do something that I might not ordinarily enjoy. His pleasure produces a different kind of reward.

Carol and Tim's experience brings out the theme of this book, an essential ingredient in avoiding sexual monotony. Each of the five senses has a part to play in imaginative lovemaking. Any creative lover can use these senses to enhance the sensuality of the moment. Carol used the smell of the candle, the taste of the wine, the feel of the condom, and the sound of the music. There are so many possibilities.

Throughout this book, I want to encourage you to use each of your senses to its fullest, to experiment in ways you may not have considered. Use everything: cold and hot, light and dark, sweet and sour, loud and soft. The smell of perfume, the taste of whipped cream (don't laugh; it's silly but fun), the sight of sexy lingerie, the sound of "dirty talk," the feel of an erotic massage can all add to your enjoyment.

There's so much to try, so much pleasure to experience if you just relax and don't always take sex seriously. Smile, giggle, be silly. Just have fun.

Each of the chapters in this book deals with the use of a single sense in lovemaking. Of course I realize that no sense stands by itself. You can't taste without using your sense of smell. Looking and touching frequently go together. But for the sake of structure, each chapter will concentrate on a single sense.

As you read, gather ideas. If you find that you're excited by an idea, try it as soon as you can. Interrupt your reading to make love to your partner. The rest of the reading can wait for another day.

A few things need to be mentioned before we start. First, as a woman, I tend to write from the woman's point of view. Little that I say, however, is in any way limited to one sex. Most of the things I discuss are applicable to either sex, so I use the words *he* and *she* interchangeably. Changing your scent applies as much to new shaving lotion as to new perfume. Tight black jockey shorts are as sexy as red lace teddies.

Honey can be poured on anyone's anatomy. Don't limit your thinking.

In addition to gender, there is the issue of your formal relationship with your partner. It's irrelevant. Throughout this book, I'll use the term *partner* to mean a person of either sex with whom you wish to make love. It is independent of whether you are married, living together, or just dating.

Another thing I need to mention is my use of four-letter words. It's impossible to write a book like this using only the words *penis* and *vagina.* And I can't stand most euphemisms such as *rod, hole, nether regions,* and *manhood.* But I also want to stay away from purely clinical terms such as *vulva* and *testes.* I hope that *fuck, cock, balls, cunt,* and *pussy* don't offend too many of you. If they do offend, maybe this book isn't for you.

A few comments about orgasm. We have been conditioned to believe that orgasm is the outcome to strive for during sex. We've been taught that foreplay is a way to get us sufficiently excited for penetration. This is ridiculous. Most of the fun can be had during the minutes or hours it takes to get to the moment the penis enters the vagina, not only during the few seconds of actual intercourse. Everything you do from the time you first get together can be part of sexual pleasure. Looking, smelling, tasting, and feeling are not means; they are ends in themselves. Savor your enjoyment.

Sometimes, as Carol found, these pleasures are enough, without an orgasm happening at all. Ed and I have made love when I know that we can't even have intercourse, usually because I have my period and I don't enjoy intercourse then. But I can hold his penis and stroke him until he comes. Have you ever felt an orgasm that way? It's fantastic to feel the pleasure you can give.

Occasionally, we make love for a second or third time in an evening and Ed's just beyond the ability to climax. That's fine also. There are so many joys apart from penetration and orgasm.

Sometimes we have intercourse and he climaxes and I don't. If I need to climax, I have learned to express my wishes. Then I masturbate while he watches, or he uses his mouth or his hands, or we use a vibrator or a dildo. Frequently, however, the power and pleasure of his climax are enough for me. I don't need any more. Climax is a choice, albeit a wonderful one.

A few words about birth control. Don't wait to think about it until the last moment. If you use the pill or are past menopause, that's wonderful. You're protected at all times. If you need to use a diaphragm or sponge, however, insert it *every* night, or morning, if you make love then. That way, your lovemaking can be spontaneous. No decisions need to be made, since you're always ready. If you use condoms, have a good supply handy. And be sure they're fresh and not dried out. A hole or tear defeats the purpose.

If you're having sex with a new partner, always use a condom. We live in the age of AIDS and any new sexual relationship is potentially deadly. You're not only having sex with a new partner but with every partner he or she has ever had. Discuss the subject beforehand. It's no longer taboo. Carry a supply yourself—whether you're a man or a woman—in case your partner is unprepared. Condoms are available everywhere. You can get them in colors, with lubricants or without, with reservoirs on the end or with studs or ribs. Don't get into a situation where you neglect protection because you're excited and your needs overwhelm your good sense.

Have fun putting the condom on as Carol and Tim did. Do it together. Enjoy the pause that allows you to come down a bit, only to soar again a moment later. Enjoy the first penetration with a cold, lubricated condom. (We'll talk more about heat and cold later. Just let me state, from enjoyable personal experience, that cold is wonderful.)

And use the condom properly. Put it on before any penis-vagina contact, before even playing. Both vaginal secretions and the fluids present before a man's ejaculation are dangerous. And keep the condom on until he is fully withdrawn. Hold it, if you have to.

Now that we have the basics understood, let's explore some new ideas and, most important, let's have some fun.

Sexual communication is a miraculous gift that you can give your partner. And if your partner begins such a dialogue, don't feel threatened. Feel delighted. Realize that someone is trying to tell you something wonderful.

2

IF IT LOOKS INTRIGUING...

Take a moment to think about the role that your sense of sight plays in your sex play. What do you think about? The loving look on your partner's face? The sight of his naked body? The vision of a movie you saw together that triggered a night of experimentation?

Let's explore. How is the room lighted when you and your partner make love? Like most couples, you probably make love at night, so it's dark outside. Usually the only light in the room comes from the lamp on your bed table. Or maybe the only light comes from the fixture in the bathroom. Or perhaps you make love in the dark.

Whatever your usual lighting, change something. Turn all the lights off or put them on. Drape a red silk kerchief over the lamp (but be careful that it doesn't touch the bulb and create a fire hazard) or get a colored light bulb. Soft yellow is nice, so is red or blue. Personally, I would shy away from green because

I think it makes everyone look ill. But if green turns you on, great.

Make love by candlelight. It really is romantic. People look softer, as if seen through an oiled lens. To avoid the danger of fire, take care that you have a good location and a secure candle holder. Protect your curtains from fire and your furniture from wax drippings.

Have your partner lie spread-eagled on the bed and turn out all the lights in the room. Then let the beam from a flashlight play over his body, highlighting each part while you tell him in great detail exactly what you're going to do to or with that part.

Make love in the daytime with the sun streaming through the window. Sunlight is wonderfully sensual and you can feel the warmth on your skin. Try positioning your partner with a shaft of sunlight on his penis. Heat on private places is an incredibly sexy feeling.

Another way to use the sense of sight is to change the way you look. Change your makeup and the way you do your nails. Wear long dangly earrings or shoes with very high heels. I used to own a pair of red shoes with four-inch heels. I occasionally wore them for an evening at home, with red or black stockings held up by a garter belt. I called it my whorehouse look and behaved accordingly. Your clothes can speak for you in the same way.

Women: Wear a tight skirt or one that's very short, hiding just enough. Wear a low-cut blouse or a bra that pushes your breasts together and creates a lot of cleavage. Or wear no bra. If you never go braless because of your lack of natural uplift, do it anyway. A little sway and jiggle is very erotic. Let your erect nipples show through an open-weave sweater or a tight polo shirt. Your partner will feel that they're just waiting to be sucked.

Men: Wear tight jeans, ones that might be too tight in the crotch or across the buns for everyday wear. With luck, you won't have them on long enough for them to become too uncomfortable. And take off your shirt. My favorite outfit for a man is jeans, just jeans with no shirt. Or wear one of those tight muscle T-shirts that show off your shoulders and upper arms. Try unbuttoning your shirt down to the navel—it worked for Harry Belafonte. Go barefoot. I think a barefoot man looks as if he is ready to jump out of his clothes and into bed.

Whatever you wear, watch for the reaction in your partner's eyes. That will be your cue as to what turns him on, so you can improve on it for the next time.

Remember the scene in *Flashdance* where Jennifer Beals changes from her going-out clothes into a loose sweatshirt with a very wide neckline? Then she takes her bra off from under the shirt. For me, that was a very erotic scene, both because of what she wore and because of that wonderful "I want to fuck your brains out" look on Michael Nouri's face. If that's the look that you would like to see on your partner's face (and who wouldn't), try something similar. Take an old shirt and cut holes in strategic places or widen the neckline so much that it keeps slipping down and revealing all sorts of wonderful parts. Cut holes in the front of a blouse so that your nipples show occasionally as you move. You can even cut the crotch out of a pair of old pants and let your pubic hair peep out. The bonus is that you can then make love with all your clothes on—a highly erotic experience.

Wear nothing but a wide leather belt and a pair of high-heeled shoes. Dress in only a slip or nothing but lots of jewelry. You get the idea. And you don't have to spend money to achieve a look you want. You may have things in the back of your closet that you've long since forgotten, or you can trade clothes with your friends. You can spend just a little on a new look by scouting garage and tag sales. What you wear doesn't have to be expensive. You merely have to be different, exciting, enticing. Let your clothes make a statement and your partner will quickly get the idea. If he's a little slow to pick up on your ideas, be patient and give him a few hints. Once he gets your message, the enjoyment begins.

You can also dress up like a character in a favorite fantasy. Help your partner understand that this is the way you'd like to be treated. You can even have an outfit ready for your partner so he can change clothes also. Then let your imagination carry you away.

In the two stories that follow, women dress up to create an illusion. In the first story, Linda uses a full peasant skirt, long earrings, and bare feet. In the second, Debbie tries a totally different approach.

LINDA AND HENRY'S STORY

Linda and Henry had spent a lot of their three-year marriage in the bedroom. From the outset of their relationship, they were kindred spirits, enjoying lovemaking at all hours of the day and night. One night, Linda told Henry about a fantasy that she had had since childhood. She said that it took place a thousand years ago. She was a paid dancing girl and whore who educated a prince about the joys of sex. As she talked about it, Linda became so excited that she almost tore Henry's clothes off. Their lovemaking that night had never been better. While she still didn't want to risk coming right out and saying so, Henry got the message that she would enjoy acting it out with him.

About a week later, Henry arrived home from work with a large box under his arm. Although Linda pestered him, he wouldn't even discuss the contents until after dinner.

When the meal was finally over, they put the dishes in the dishwasher, refilled their wineglasses, and went into the bedroom. Henry handed the box to Linda and watched her face as she opened it.

Inside was a costume Henry had rented. There was a red peasant blouse and a full multicolored skirt. In a separate package was a large, gaudy necklace and a pair of earrings that were actually tiny bells.

"I want you to put those on," Henry said. "Then we'll play."

Linda was too shocked to speak. Embarrassed but excited, she took the packages into the bathroom to change.

Five minutes later, Linda came back into the bedroom. She was dressed as a dancing girl, her breasts almost spilling out of the neckline of the low-cut blouse. The necklace hung heavily between her breasts and the earrings jingled as she moved. She had added an old bracelet on one bare ankle and had adjusted her makeup to match the mood she was creating. She had even put a quick coat of bright red polish on her nails.

Henry spent a full minute letting his eyes roam over his wife's exotic body. "You look terrific," he said, and he patted the bed next to him. "Now sit here by me and I'll tell you a story."

Linda sat down on the bed next to her husband and curled her bare feet under her.

"Once upon a time in a faraway land," Henry began, his voice low and seductive, "there lived a prince named Henry who wanted above all to learn to be a good king. He spent a considerable amount of time wandering through his kingdom in disguise, getting to know his subjects. He wanted to understand what they wanted and needed from their king."

Henry had rehearsed the whole plot for days, and from Linda's rapt attention and heavy breathing, he knew his story was right on target. He sipped his wine, then continued.

"One evening, Prince Henry arrived at an inn on the outskirts of a small city. It had been a long trip and he was tired and hungry, so he decided to have dinner and stay at the inn for the night. As he looked around the inn's common room, he appreciated that, like most of the public houses in the kingdom, it was clean and well kept.

"He found the innkeeper, a short, bald man with a huge belly, and told him to pour him a drink and bring him a portion of whatever meat he had available. Then Prince Henry sat at a little table in the corner of the room and drank the tankard of ale the inn-keeper had poured for him. It was not unusual that no one recognized him, dressed as he was in the clothes of a wandering laborer."

Henry paused.

"Don't stop now," Linda said.

"I have no intention of stopping," Henry said. He took another sip of his wine.

"A good meal and a good night's sleep are just what I need, Prince Henry thought. When the inn-keeper's daughter appeared, however, Henry started to think about more than just a meal and sleep. The girl was startlingly beautiful. Her long black hair fell over one shoulder and curled around the bottom of her full breast. Her tawny skin was clearly visible above the low neckline of her bright red peasant blouse and her hips made her many-colored skirt sway from side to side. Her soft blue eyes sparkled when she looked at him."

Henry paused in his storytelling and looked at Linda. "She looked just like you do now." He kissed her on her full lips, then sat back and resumed his story.

"The girl crossed the room and placed a plate of venison stew in front of Prince Henry. As she did so, she bent over deeply and allowed him a good view of the tops of her large breasts."

Henry looked at his wife on the bed next to him. "What do you think she said then?"

Linda smiled and hesitated only a moment. "I'm glad to be of service," she said, playing the part of the girl.

"And what is your name?" Henry said, lowering the pitch of his voice to play the part of the prince.

"My name is Linda," she said in a deep, throaty voice. "What's yours?"

"Henry," he said. "What do you do here all evening?"

"I serve my father's stew and sometimes, though not tonight, I dance for the customers." Linda licked her lips and gazed into her husband's eyes. "Sometimes I also provide other forms of entertainment." She winked at him.

With his arm around his wife's shoulder and his mouth close to her ear, Henry picked up the story.

"Prince Henry felt his penis begin to swell under his breeches, but he suppressed the urge to throw the beautiful girl on the floor and fuck her right then and there. He had tumbled his share of wenches, but those experiences had always been quick fucks with sweet young palace maids. Linda looked as if she would certainly be able to provide interesting entertainment. 'You're a pretty little thing,' he said, pinching her bottom."

As Henry continued the tale, his wife sat up a bit straighter and arched her back. There was now a saucy tilt to her head and a gleam in her eyes. Henry slid his hand under his wife's bottom and squeezed one cheek.

Henry slipped back into Prince Henry's voice. "What kind of entertainment can you provide, pretty Linda?"

Linda picked up the story. "If you've a few copper coins, we could do whatever you want."

Her husband took his cue. "Prince Henry hesitated only an instant. He pulled a handful of coins from his pocket and counted a few into her hand. 'These are for the meal,' he said. Then he poured the rest into her other hand. 'And these are for you.'"

Linda turned and, in her dancing-girl voice, whispered into her husband's ear. "Finish your dinner and I'll finish up my duties down here. I'll meet you in your room in about an hour."

The storytelling continued. "To kill time, Prince Henry ate his stew, although he had little appetite for it. While Henry ate, he watched Linda serve the few customers. He watched the impudent swish of her skirts and her bare ankles. He watched her breasts bounce under her blouse. A few times, she looked back at him and thrust her chest forward so he could see the outline of her nipples through the fabric."

Linda thrust her chest forward. Henry tweaked his wife's nipples so they stood out under the sheer material of her blouse.

"Prince Henry wanted to see Linda dance, but he was glad that she wasn't dancing this evening. Dancing would take a long time and he didn't want to wait for her. He finished his stew and half a loaf of bread, washed them down with the rest of his ale, and made his way up to his room."

Henry paused and looked at his wife. He knew she wasn't ready for overt actions yet. "Would you dance for me some evening?"

As Linda nodded, Henry smiled and resumed the story. "Prince Henry's room was a simple one: a large bed with a soft mattress, a trunk for his clothes, and a table on which stood a small lamp, a water pitcher, and a bowl. Henry lighted the lamp and turned it low. Then he pulled off his boots and settled on the bed to wait."

Henry rose from the bed and crossed to the dresser. He lighted a small candle and extinguished all the lights in the room. He continued his story. "Only a few minutes later, the door opened and Linda walked in. She crossed the room and sat down on the bed."

At this point, Henry and his wife began to act out the scene. Henry reached up and slid his hand around to the back of Linda's neck. Then he pulled her face down and pressed his lips against hers. She was soft and warm and gave promise of delights to come.

She parted her lips and teased the tip of Henry's tongue with her own. She sucked gently, pulling his tongue inside the warmth of her mouth.

Henry was surprised. She felt like a different person. It was almost like making love to a whore, but the woman was his wife.

As they kissed, Linda stroked Henry's chest through his shirt. She felt the firm muscles of his shoulders and upper arms. While her hands touched him, Henry kneaded Linda's back and moved his hands sensuously up and down her neck and spine. He pressed the small of her back and felt her pliant body against the length of him.

Minutes later, Henry wound his hand in Linda's hair and pulled her face away. With his other hand, he reached down the top of her low-cut blouse and pulled one breast free. He gazed at the large globe in his hand, tipped by her dark brown nipple, already swollen and reaching toward his mouth.

The married couple in their bedroom in suburbia had become the prince and the whore, somewhere in an ancient inn.

Henry could not resist the temptation of his wife's breast. He took it in his mouth and flicked his tongue over the swollen tip. He felt it grow even harder as he swirled his tongue over her dark flesh. He drew her breast into his mouth and stroked it with the palm of his hand. He massaged her upper back, which pushed her breast more firmly into his mouth.

He sucked, drawing her nipple deep into his mouth, then releasing the pressure. Over and over, he sucked and released as he felt her body throb against his. He felt her tremble as she reached for the back of his head, holding him tighter against her chest. He released one breast, only to repeat his sucking on the other. He felt her hips begin to move rhythmically.

Slowly, he drew away. He sat up and gently pulled Linda's blouse up over her head, leaving the necklace to hang heavily between her breasts. Her flesh almost glowed as he caressed her with his eyes.

"You have a magnificent body, Linda," Henry

murmured, in character as the prince. "Let me see all of you."

"Certainly, sir." She stood up and pulled off her skirt, and he saw that she was wearing nothing underneath. She stood next to the bed, naked except for her necklace and earrings and the bracelet around her ankle.

His eyes roamed her voluptuous body. Her breasts were full, her nipples erect. Her ribs were narrow and hips slender. Her long and shapely legs were topped by a V of curly dark hair.

She slid her hands over her body and under her breasts, offering them to him.

"Oh yes," Henry said as he stood up. "I want what you're offering. I want you very much." He quickly removed his clothes, lay back down, and pulled Linda down beside him. His eyes and hands traveled over her body freely. Then his lips followed his hands. He tasted her skin. He licked and kissed and nipped at her chest and belly, her arms and her ribs.

He brushed his fingertips lightly across the top of her pubic bush and watched her skin react to his touch. Her back arched and stretched, inviting his touch on her vagina. His mouth and fingers were almost everywhere, but he was in no hurry to touch her between her legs.

He turned her over and kissed her spine. He moved his tongue over the sensitive spot in the small of her back and over the mounds of her ass. He blew on the wet flesh. Tiny cries escaped her mouth.

His mouth traveled down the backs of her thighs to the backs of her knees, where he placed tiny bites.

Her body was going crazy. She thrashed so much that he had to hold her ankles to allow him to continue his exploration.

He turned her over on her back.

He felt the heat radiating from her and slid his hand from her belly to the soaked folds between her legs. Her body was wide open for him, drawing him nearer. She raised her knees and opened her thighs wide.

He stroked her with his hand and his mouth devoured hers. He swirled his tongue in her mouth in the same rhythm as his fingers moved in the cleft between her legs.

Suddenly, Linda was no longer satisfied with her passive posture. In the fantasy, she was a whore, knowledgeable and creative. She wanted to show her "prince" the joys of love. She looked down and saw her long fingers with their bright red polish. These were the hands of the whore in the story, not the housewife. She reached her hand down between their bodies and grasped his erect penis with her long fingers. He gasped at the heat her hand caused. Passion flowed through his body, adding his heat to hers.

Henry was surprised and pleased at his wife's aggression. In the past, she had usually been the passive partner, willing to do whatever they enjoyed, but never the initiator. Now she was the active one.

At first, she just held his erection and squeezed slightly. Then she pulled, putting some tension in her grasp. Her squeezing and pulling took on the rhythm of his stroking until his hunger was as great as hers. She pulled away until his hand slipped from her body while her hand continued to draw on his cock. Her body began to move against him, with the rhythm of her hand on his cock trapped between them.

She knew he was about to come when she felt him try to roll on top of her. She pressed him down on the bed. "No," she said hoarsely, "Linda the whore wants to pleasure you her way."

Henry reveled in his wife's new role. He soon lost control of his body and his mind. Her hand was all that he could think about.

She continued to fuck him with her hand. She rubbed and squeezed his cock while she reached for his testicles with her other hand. She ran the tips of her fingers over his balls and across the heated skin at the base of his cock.

"Yes," she said as she felt the contractions in his balls, "come for me. Let Linda watch you."

He looked up and saw that her face was consumed with passion. As she swayed in rhythm with her hand, her necklace caught the light and the bells on her earrings tinkled.

When she slid her finger back and touched his puckered anus, he could wait no more. All thoughts faded and he felt his semen press upward. Totally out of control, he spewed his juices across her hands and his belly.

"You're a witch," he said, breathless. A moment later, he continued, "But I'm not done with Linda yet."

If she would do that to him, he would return the favor. He pressed her onto her back on the bed and plunged two fingers inside her vagina, fucking her with his hand. He pulled out and plunged deeply again. She responded swiftly and her hips fucked his hand. He reached down with his other hand and touched the center of her hunger. He had seldom seen her so hot.

"More," she screamed, "I want more inside of me."

Henry added a third finger to the two already thrusting in and out of her hot cunt.

"Yes. Now," she yelled. "Do it now."

As she had, he touched her anus. She came as he massaged her ass and her cunt. Her muscles squeezed the fingers inside of her. Her hips bucked and her thighs held his hands against her fevered flesh. Over and over, she thrust her hips up against his hands.

They held each other until their bodies were calm. Linda sighed. Somehow she wanted to complete the fantasy. She looked up at Henry through lowered lashes and smiled. "I have to go now or my father will begin to wonder where I am." Her rich, throaty laugh filled the room. "He doesn't mind what I do with the customers as long as I finish my work in the kitchen."

Henry reached over and pulled his wallet from his bedside table. He withdrew some bills. "Here, wench." He laughed. "Give these to your father. And thank him for your *services*."

DEBBIE'S STORY

Debbie and her husband, Jay, had been married for six years and their sex life had never been better. They experimented with varied scenarios, telling stories and then acting them out. They were both creative and willing to take risks.

Jay's stories had recently centered on kidnapping a young girl and taking her to his mountain cabin. While Jay stroked her, he would tell the story of what happened to the poor virgin as he tied her up and introduced her to the mysteries of sex. They had even bought soft fur-lined straps for Debbie's wrists and ankles and he occasionally tied her to the bed. She got hungry as she remembered the night they had first tried them out.

One afternoon, Debbie was reading an article about changing her sexual image when the idea hit her. Why not? she thought. She put the magazine on the table and allowed her mind to wander. Yes, she realized as she mentally inventoried her wardrobe, she had everything she needed right in the house.

That evening, Debbie and Jay had dinner and watched a movie that Jay had rented. After the movie, while Jay watched the local news, Debbie disappeared into the bathroom. First, she used makeup remover, then washed her face to clean off all traces of the day's eye shadow and blush. Then she brushed her long brown hair and braided it into two long plaits that hung down and brushed the tops of her small breasts.

Earlier in the day, she had hidden the outfit she wanted to wear in the bathroom hamper and now she pulled the clothes out. She dressed in a white cotton bra that she had found pushed to the back of a dresser drawer and white cotton underpants. Then she added a plain white blouse, a plaid skirt, high socks, and white sneakers. When she looked at herself in the mirror, she had to admit that, despite her twenty-nine years, she now looked like an old-fashioned, very prim high school girl.

She took a deep breath and walked down the hall and into the living room. Jay was still sitting on the sofa, his long legs stretched out on the coffee table. "Excuse me, sir," Debbie said, "could you tell me how to get to Broadway and Main Street? I'm going to surprise my aunt with a visit but I seem to have gotten lost."

Jay stared for a moment, then suddenly understood. She had begun one of his favorite fantasies. "Certainly, dear," he said, "I can even drive you, if you'd like."

Debbie giggled. This was so silly, and so exciting. "That would be so kind of you." She sat down on the sofa next to Jay and primly kept her knees together as her short skirt rode up her naked thighs. After a moment, she looked around and said, "Excuse me, sir, but I don't recognize any landmarks. Are we going the right way?"

"I'm taking a slightly longer route, but I thought you'd enjoy the scenery." Jay had slipped completely into the fantasy and he found that he was getting very excited. He took a deep breath to calm down. "You know," he said, "you may be right about the directions. Here we are at my house. I have a map inside and we could check for the location of your aunt's house."

Slightly self-consciously, Debbie and Jay got up and

walked down the hallway to their bedroom, in search of "the map." Each was having the same reaction, excitement spiced with the urge to laugh.

Debbie preceded Jay into the bedroom, then Jay loudly slammed the door behind her. He looked at her and smiled. "Now I have you," he said, an exaggerated leer lighting his face. "You're here in my cabin and there's no way out."

Debbie rearranged her face and tried to look like a frightened girl. "I d-d-don't understand. What are you g-g-going to do?" It was amazing to Debbie that, although she was a grown woman, she was feeling some of the things that the girl in the fantasy might be feeling.

"We're going to have some fun. I love initiating beautiful girls into the ways of love."

Debbie's urge to laugh almost overcame her at that moment, but she suppressed it. She knew that there was nothing wrong with a good laugh, but she didn't want to break the spell of this moment. "You mean sex?" she said.

"Exactly, sweet thing. Tell me, have you ever been with a man?"

Debbie tried to look horrified. "Never. It's very bad. I would never..."

Swiftly, Jay grabbed Debbie's wrist and twisted it behind her as he pulled her close. His mouth came down hard on hers. As he kissed her, she stayed in character and kept her lips tightly closed. After a moment, he pulled back. "Open your mouth!" he snapped.

"But you're hurting me," she cried, struggling against

his strength, but not hard enough that there was a chance she'd get away.

"Do as you're told!" Jay said. He knew that her cries were merely part of the fantasy. They had agreed long before that if either of them wanted to stop any activity at any time, they only had to say, "I'm serious, please stop." Jay pressed his mouth against hers. Slowly, she parted her lips and his tongue roughly explored her dark cavern. When he finally leaned back, he said softly, "You're just as sweet as I thought you'd be."

Without releasing her wrist, he opened the bed table's drawer, where their "toys" were kept. "Now, I'll just assure your complete cooperation." He pulled out the furry restraints, threw Debbie onto the bed, and quickly tied her wrists and ankles to the four corners. Debbie struggled just enough to keep Jay's job from being too easy.

When he had her tied, still fully clothed, he stepped back. "Now, sweet thing, let's see what you have on under those school clothes."

"Oh, please, mister," Debbie protested, "I'm a good girl. Please don't hurt me."

"Hurt you?" Jay said. "I have no intention of hurting you. I told you. We're just going to have some fun." Slowly, Jay unbuttoned Debbie's white blouse and pulled it open. He grinned when he saw her plain white bra. It was just like Debbie to make the illusion complete down to her underwear. She was so terrific.

Jay was amazed at how much he wanted to see Debbie's "virginal breasts." He had undressed his wife hundreds of times, but it had never felt like this. He pushed his index finger under the center of the bra and flipped it up over Debbie's breasts. He leaned down and hungrily sucked at her nipples. "You see, sweet thing," he said between sucks, "how hard your nipples become when I suck them?"

"Please," Debbie cried as Jay's mouth fastened on her nipple, "don't do that. It's so bad. Only bad girls would let a man do that."

Jay sat on the edge of the bed, his hands kneading and pinching his wife's breasts. "I'm going to do a lot more to you before this evening is finished."

Debbie continued to struggle. She wiggled her body around to the extent that the bonds allowed, closed her eyes, and thrashed her head from side to side. "Let me up! Oh please, let me up!" She managed to put a catch in her voice, as if she was really trying not to cry.

Jay continued to squeeze her breasts as she tried vainly to escape. Here he was in his ultimate dream. He was a ravisher of virgins. He smiled. He had never had any doubt that his thoughts about making love to a nubile young thing had nothing to do with any desire actually to do it. The idea existed only in his fantasy world, and now he and his wife were making his dream real.

When she quieted, he said, "Are you through fighting me, sweet thing? You can't get away, and I wouldn't want you to injure yourself." Debbie opened her eyes wide and stared at Jay. They were both so hot, she realized. This fantasy had proved to be better than she had ever imagined.

"That's a good girl," Jay crooned. He looked at his

wife stretched out on the bed, her skirt rucked up around her waist. "Now, I want to see and touch all of you, and you better not fight. I'm going to untie your ankles for a moment, but just stay still."

Debbie had no intention of moving.

Jay released her ankles and quickly removed her skirt and panties. As he tossed her white cotton undies onto the floor, he noticed that the crotch was soaked. She's as into this as I am, he realized. He started to pull off her high socks, then changed his mind and left them in place. They add to the illusion, he thought.

"I want to explore your body," he said. He pulled the straps attached to her ankles up between her legs and forced her knees to bend. He tied the straps to the headboard of the bed and looked at his creation.

Debbie's knees were raised and spread wide apart. She watched Jay stare at her pussy, wet, open, and available. Somehow, she felt vulnerable and deliciously violated so she tried to press her legs together. They were stopped by the straps between her thighs and by Jay's hand on her knee. "Don't," he said, his voice hoarse. She allowed her knees to fall open.

For a while, Jay simply stared at his wife's "virginal" body. Then he used his index finger to explore the folds between Debbie's legs. "You're so wet," he said. "You must be a very bad girl to get so wet."

"I'm a good girl," Debbie whined. "You're the one who's bad."

Jay laughed. "You're right. I'm very bad and I'm going to do very bad things to you." He reached into the toy drawer and pulled out Debbie's favorite large flesh-colored dildo. "We're just going to see what a bad girl you are. I'm going to push this big toy prick deep inside of you, sweet thing," he said. "Only a bad girl would enjoy it, and you will enjoy it. Your hips will move and you'll beg me to keep fucking you. Then I'll know how bad you really are."

"You wouldn't do that."

"Just watch me." He laughed deep in his throat. "No, I guess you can't watch, tied up that way, but you can feel." He rubbed the plastic against her cunt until it was wet and slippery, then slowly pushed the toy deep into his wife's body. He gradually withdrew it, then pushed it in again. He watched as her eyes closed and her breathing quickened. Her hips began to move in rhythm with his strokes. "Do you want me to stop now, sweet thing?"

When Debbie remained silent, Jay stopped his movements. "Do you want me to stop, my bad little girl?"

"No," Debbie whispered.

"Only a bad girl would want me to continue. Tell me you want me to continue." He moved the dildo in short strokes, then stopped again.

"It's so bad to want that."

"I know, but you do and you will ask me to continue."

After a long silence, Debbie finally said, "Please, don't stop."

Jay slid the dildo deep inside of her, then pulled it out. He used long, slow strokes to drive Debbie to the edge. "You're going to make me come if you do that," Debbie cried, slipping out of character.

"Not just yet." Jay left the dildo in Debbie's cunt, then swiftly removed his pants and untied her ankles.

He slowly pulled the dildo out of her soaked pussy and replaced it with his fully erect penis.

Her arms still tied above her head, Debbie could only wrap her legs around Jay's waist and press her hips against his. "Don't stop fucking me," she yelled, now completely out of character but very hungry. "Don't stop."

Jay pounded for only a moment until they came almost simultaneously. As he collapsed, he pulled at the slipknots he had tied and released Debbie's arms. "Holy shit," he said. "That was incredible."

"It's never been better," Debbie said, knowing that it was true. "That fantasy made me as hot as it obviously made you."

"Fantasy?" Jay said in mock horror. "You mean you weren't a virgin?"

Debbie and Jay laughed and then, each still partly clothed, fell asleep.

Another way to use your sense of sight is to watch your lovemaking. Keep your eyes open and look at your partner. Watch his enjoyment and revel in it. Watch his face to see his reactions to new things that you try. He may be unwilling or unable to say "It's wonderful" or "It's not my taste," but his face usually will.

Use mirrors to watch yourself and your partner while you make love. If you wish, move a big mirror into a position so you both can see. Just be careful that it's well supported so that it doesn't fall when things get active. If you're thinking about having your bedroom ceiling mirrored, you probably should have it done professionally. Glass suspended above me, threatening to fall and do serious injury, would scare me to death unless it was hung by someone who knew exactly what he was doing.

You can derive tremendous pleasure by watching your partner give herself pleasure. Betsy always knew she enjoyed it when men looked at her. One afternoon, when she least expected it, she had a wonderful idea on how to enhance her lovemaking with her husband, Don. She didn't hesitate to act on it.

BETSY'S STORY

Betsy loved the way men stared at her. She took pride in her small, tight body with its tiny pink-nippled breasts. She easily dismissed the idea that men only like women with big tits. Ridiculous. She was convinced that men love to look at women, any kind, especially those who love to be looked at. And so she dressed for men and expected them to take notice.

Don loved the way she attracted stares from men. "They can look," he said frequently, "but they can't touch." He had no doubt that Betsy was faithful.

One afternoon, Betsy was wandering through her neighborhood mall with her three children. They walked through Sears while Betsy looked for new towels for the bathroom. While in the Bed and Bath section, she spotted a transparent plastic shower curtain. She looked at it, then stopped, stood stock-still, and stared out into space, her brain clicking. "What's up, Mom?" her nine-year-old asked.

"Nothing, darling, nothing at all," she said, pulling herself back to earth. She grabbed the shower curtain and quickly paid for it. Grinning, she left the store and hurried to her car, urging her children to keep pace. At home, she rushed into the master bathroom, removed the old shower curtain, and put up the new one. She climbed into the dry tub and pulled the curtain flat in the middle so that the folds were at the ends, pleased that she could see quite clearly through the transparent plastic.

That evening, the family had dinner and, after what seemed to Betsy to be an interminably long evening, the children went to bed.

"Don," Betsy called, "I want to take a shower. Why don't you come into the bathroom and talk with me while I do. We've had no chance to visit in days."

Visiting in the bathroom was not an unusual request, since moments when they could spend time just talking were few and far between. "Sure," he responded, "let me get a beer."

As Don walked down the hall toward the bedroom with his beer, he heard the shower start. He walked through the bedroom, into the bathroom, and sat down on the closed toilet seat. Paying no attention to the shower, he put his beer down on the vanity. "How was your day, darling?" he asked.

"Fine, and yours?"

Don took a breath to begin the story of an unpleasant encounter with his boss and turned toward the shower. "What in the world?" He could see Betsy's back through the shower curtain. His boss forgotten, he watched the water cascade over her shoulders, down her spine, and between her cheeks.

Her back to Don, Betsy rubbed her hands on the soap until she had lots of lather. "You mean the curtain?" she said with mock innocence. "I bought it today. Like it?" She slowly turned so Don could see her whole body. Deliberately, she rubbed the lather over her flat belly.

"Ummmm" was all Don could say as the water poured down Betsy's breasts. "Very lovely."

Betsy's hands made small circles over her stomach and down the front of her thighs. She turned and let the water flow over her and felt the rivulets of soapy water run down her legs.

She glanced over at Don and saw that his eyes were riveted on her hands. She picked up the soap and again rubbed it into a thick lather. Slowly, she lifted her hands and rubbed her soapy palms over her flat breasts. She felt her nipples harden under her hands until they stood out from her chest like mountains. She let her head fall back and for long minutes she massaged her breasts with her slippery hands. Knowing that Don was watching just enhanced her pleasure.

She again turned to the shower and let the water spray over her chest and belly. She was both hot and cold, hot from the water and the heat her flesh was generating, cold from the cool air as the water evaporated from her skin where the shower didn't reach.

"You're very quiet," she murmured.

"I'm enjoying the show," Don said. "Please, don't stop now."

Betsy again lathered her hands and rubbed them on her ribs and down over her flat abdomen. With each circle, her fingers slipped closer to her pubic hair until she was rubbing her mound with each stroke.

"God, you're so beautiful," Don said. He unzipped his pants and let his hard cock spring free. "Touch yourself while I watch," he said, his voice thick.

"And you, too," Betsy said. She stared through the curtain as Don's hands began to stroke his erection. As she watched him, she let her hands slide into the slippery flesh between her legs. Her fingers found her swollen clit and she began to rub it. Every few strokes, she let her finger slide backward between her swollen lips.

She lifted her foot and pushed the shower curtain up so she could place her toes on the rim of the tub. While she rubbed her vagina, she watched Don stroke his cock.

"It's so good," she said, massaging her swollen clit and breathing hard.

"It's wonderful," Don said, rubbing more quickly.

"Oh yes. Oh yes," they said almost simultaneously as they came.

As Don used a facecloth to clean up, Betsy rinsed herself off and stepped out of the tub. Her knees could hardly hold her up but she stood still while Don dried every inch of her body with a large, fluffy towel.

Don quickly stripped off his clothes and together they climbed into bed. Holding each other tightly, they relived the delicious experience they had shared.

As they talked, they found they were both excited again, so Don pulled Betsy over on top of him and drove his cock into her until they both came again.

Amazed, Betsy said, "Twice in one night? It's been so long since we made love twice in one night. That shower curtain must have really gotten you excited."

"Just thinking about the way you looked is unbelievably exciting." Don giggled. "If you could find some transparent towels to go with the curtain, maybe next time we could try for three."

We can't leave the subject of the power of sight without talking about photographs. Decades ago, "naughty" postcards and nudie photographs were treasured, passed from father to son, from man to man. The view of a female body—sometimes dressed in a skimpy outfit, sometimes totally nude—formed the basis of many a fantasy.

Men visited strip shows in seedy neighborhoods to look at bare breasts and exposed pubic hair. The shows were seldom creative, but creativity wasn't necessary. The only requirement was a host of naked female bodies.

Although postcards and strip shows still exist, they are much less necessary than they once were. Now there are magazines and videos for almost any taste and almost any fantasy. You can watch women with huge breasts, well-built men with oiled biceps, nude fat ladies, men with cocks that reach unbelievable lengths, woman having sexual relations with other women, men with men, threesomes, foursomes, and more-somes, and on and on and on as often as you like.

And, of course, there's TV's Playboy channel. A friend of mine describes it as "Sesame Street" for adults, and that's not a bad characterization. Vivid colors, short film takes with exotic photography, even dancing popcorn bags before the movies. But what's wrong with that? Where "Sesame Street" is educational fun for children, the Playboy channel is erotic fun for adults. Maybe for some, it's even educational.

There's more to pictures than watching, however. Have you ever tried making your own videotape? Have you ever considered acting out your own fantasy before the camera and then playing it over and over. Naughty? Yes. And delicious. Besides showing movement, video has another advantage over still photos. Since it doesn't have to be developed, it never leaves your hands and no one else ever sees what goes on...unless you want to share your video with another couple.

How do you go about making your own tape? There are several ways. The only requirement is a video camera. Of course, they're still fairly expensive, but if you don't already own one and can't afford one, there are several options. If you know of someone who owns one, borrow it. Make some excuse if you don't want to admit that you're making an "adult" video. And if you don't know anyone who has a camera, you can rent one.

So you have a camera, now what? There are several approaches. First, one of you can hold the camera while your partner assumes sexy poses and touches

and strokes her own body. Watch your wife masturbate, film it, then show it while you both watch. Once
you get over the awkward feeling of watching yourself, it is a tremendous turn-on. Then trade places and
do it again. Of course, the moviemaking may be so
exciting that you have to wait for another night. What
could be better?

Play director. Give your partner instructions. Say "Turn
this way" or "Touch yourself there, this way." Giving or
being given instructions can be a turn-on in itself.

Another way to make a sexy movie is to prop the
camera next to the bed, using a tripod if you have
one, then make love or act out a fantasy while the
tape runs. You'll find that you slip out of the frame
from time to time, but you'll be having too much fun
to really care.

There is another way to make a videotape, but it is
for truly liberated lovers. You need a third person,
someone who can take the pictures while you and
your partner frolic. In the story that follows, another
couple helps Andy and Rita make a tape. This is an
activity for the uninhibited, but you may be more
adventuresome than you realize.

ANDY AND RITA'S STORY

Rita and Andy had gotten a video camera as a family
gift the previous Christmas. Over the following few

months, they took several tapes of their children and their vacation. Then one evening after a few beers, they made a tape of themselves. First there were about five minutes of Rita stripping slowly and sensuously for the camera, then tentatively touching herself, feeling a little awkward and very silly.

Since "Turn about is fair play," Rita filmed Andy in much the same way. They had wanted to tape some lovemaking, but they couldn't figure out how to arrange the camera.

When she rewound the tape and played it on their TV, Rita was horrified. I look so fat, she thought. Of course, television adds ten pounds, but still, I look truly fat—and not too pretty. And the whole thing was silly to begin with.

When they got to Andy's section, Rita had to admit that he didn't look badly. It was kind of sexy, watching him undress in front of the camera, then looking over and seeing him next to her. It was as if he was the star of a soft-core film like the ones they occasionally rented. As a matter of fact, watching Andy flex his muscles and then lightly touch his erection made her very excited.

Andy's reaction was much the same as Rita's, so as the tape finished, they could hardly wait to pounce on each other. Over the next few weeks, they watched the tape several more times and each time made wild love afterward. They also talked about how to make a real tape of their lovemaking, but although they tried once or twice, they couldn't work out the logistics.

A few weeks later, Rita and Andy were spending an

evening with their next-door neighbors Sue and Mark, a couple they had known since high school. The four of them had always been very close and had even done some nude swimming in Sue and Mark's pool. The children had long since gone to bed and, sitting in Andy and Rita's living room, they had all consumed more alcohol than usual.

As it did frequently, the talk turned to sex and, much to Rita's amazement, Andy casually mentioned their videotape.

"You, too?" Mark said. "We made one about a year ago and we still play it occasionally."

Relieved that Sue and Mark were kindred spirits, Andy said, "We wanted to make a tape of us making love but we had all kinds of problems. Did you figure out how to get both of you into the frame? We tried a few setups but nothing seems to work."

"Nah," Mark said. "We have a great tape of Sue masturbating for the camera, but that's about it."

"Mark!" Sue giggled. "You shouldn't talk about that."

"Want to see my tape?" Andy asked. He looked at his wife. "Could I play it, Rita? Would you mind?"

Rita blushed. She wasn't sure that she wanted anyone to see the tape, but after another drink and a lot of persuasion, she agreed. "Not in the living room," she said. "I'd die if the children walked in. Let's go into the bedroom and we can watch there."

They each grabbed a fresh beer and the four friends trooped up the stairs. Mark flopped down in the middle of the king-sized bed and motioned Rita to one side and Sue to the other. Andy turned on the TV and inserted the tape. The four were silent while they watched the tape.

"Wow," Mark said when the tape ended. He looked at Rita. "I had forgotten how gorgeous you are naked."

"Thanks," Rita answered, trying not to blush. She turned to Sue, looking for any signs of jealousy, but she saw none.

"It's all right," Sue said, catching Rita's look. "And I agree with him. You really look great. You should see our tape. I look so fat."

Rita burst out laughing and confessed that was her first impression when she looked at herself.

"Hey," Mark said. "Why don't I make a tape of the two of you making love, then you can take one of Sue and me."

"I don't know," Andy said, hesitating. "I'd love to have a tape like that, but I don't think I could make love with someone watching."

"Me, neither," Rita said quickly.

"I could close my eyes during the good parts if you want," Mark said, laughing.

"I don't know. What do you think, Rita?" Andy asked. "I'd really love to have a tape of us making it."

Rita wanted to object, but the words wouldn't come out of her mouth. She had to admit to herself that the idea sounded erotic and very exciting. She didn't know whether she could make love with other people watching, but maybe....

When Rita didn't protest, Andy rushed to the closet and pulled out the camera. "You know how to do this," he told Mark. "Just aim, press here, and the camera does the rest."

Andy quickly stretched out on the bed beside Rita and, not giving her time to change her mind, kissed her deeply. Without disturbing them, Sue got off the bed and stood beside her husband and the camera.

While Mark aimed the camera, Andy quickly undressed and removed Rita's clothes. As he began to suck on her engorged nipples, Rita, still too disconcerted by the presence of the camera to do anything, closed her eyes and self-consciously held Andy's head while he sucked.

"Relax, Rita," Mark said. "You and Andy aren't doing anything that Sue and I haven't done hundreds of times." When Rita didn't react, Mark said, "I'll be the director. Now, Andy, stroke her breasts while you suck. Knead her lovely tits."

Andy did as he was told, swirling his fingers over Rita's breasts.

"Rita," Mark continued, "caress Andy's shoulders. Make love to him with your hands." When she did, Mark said, "That's good, very good. Now kiss. I want to see your mouths devour each other."

Andy was surprised how exciting it was to listen to a friend direct their lovemaking. While Andy and Rita kissed, Mark used the zoom to tighten in on their mouths. "Ummm," Mark said, "wonderful."

As she kissed Andy with him stretched out partly on top of her, Rita felt her body relax. There was something comfortable about not having to make any decisions about lovemaking. Mark was directing and she only had to follow his instructions.

"Now, Rita, while you're kissing, fondle Andy's ass."

Rita reached down and touched Andy's cheeks.

"That's good, now use your fingernails."

Rita had never done anything like that before, but this was a night for firsts. She had very long nails, so she very lightly scratched Andy's skin. Instantly, she felt Andy's reaction. His hard cock twitched against her thigh.

She scratched him again, harder this time. Again his body reacted, this time with his hips thrusting against her.

"That's good, Rita. Andy likes it, too." Mark was totally absorbed in his role as director. He moved the camera over the other couple's bodies, panning in and pulling back. He and Sue were into a bit of rough play and he had seen Andy's reaction to Rita's fingernails, so he tried some slightly spicier direction.

"Rita, slap Andy's ass."

Rita started to pull her mouth away from Andy's to complain, but he wouldn't let her. Was he trying to tell her to do what Mark had suggested? She wasn't sure, but she raised her hand and brought it down on Andy's ass.

Andy's back arched and he said, "Oh God, Rita." Then, without any preliminaries, he thrust his cock into her. He came almost immediately.

Between gasping breaths, he said, "I'm sorry, baby, but it was all too much for me."

Rita smiled and said, "It certainly was." She turned to Mark. "Do you have all that on film?"

Mark grinned. "I sure do. It was sensational. Now, if you don't mind, I think I'll go home and attack my wife."

"Not if I attack you first," Sue said as they almost

ran out of Andy and Rita's bedroom. "Tomorrow night," she called over her shoulder, "our place. Bring the camera."

"Absolutely," Andy called.

As they heard the front door slam, Rita said, "I think it's time to watch our tape, if you're not too tired. I'm still unsatisfied."

Andy smiled. "Just give me a few minutes and I'm sure we can work something out."

3

IF IT SOUNDS SWEET...

Almost three hundred years ago, William Congreve said, "Music hath charms to soothe the savage breast." But I think we all know that soothing isn't the only thing that music does.

Music excites. I remember that when I was in my teens, there was a secret, supposedly passed on from one horny young man to another. It was said that one particular series of classical musical selections was guaranteed to make your date surrender. All I ever found out—and maybe all that ever existed—was that the series culminated with Ravel's *Bolero*. If you've ever heard that particular selection, you won't doubt the wisdom of finishing with it. The pounding beat and repeating erotic melody alone are enough to arouse. Remember Bo Derek and Dudley Moore in "*10*"?

Music can also trigger memories of wonderful times together. Barry Manilow summed it up very well when he said, "Maybe the old songs will bring back the old times." Whether songs from your past or new ones that will create memories for the future, any kind of music makes a sweet backdrop to lovemaking. I begin to think sexy thoughts whenever I hear Grieg's First Piano Concerto. It played in the background one of the first times that Ed and I made love, on the floor in front of his fireplace.

Although background music may be the thing we think of first when we think about the sense of hearing, it isn't the only way that sound can be used to enhance lovemaking. Four-letter words, spoken at an auspicious moment, arouse many people. *Cock, fuck,* and *cunt* may sound grating in ordinary conversation, but in the heat of passion the phrase "I want to feel your big, hard prick inside of me," or "I love to suck your titties" can be just the stimulus needed to raise the level of sexual intensity one more notch. Try a sentence in the heat of passion and feel your partner's reaction.

Or tell your partner in detail about your lovemaking as Kyle did.

KYLE AND LIZ'S STORY

One evening, Kyle, dressed in his pajama bottoms, and his wife, Liz, in her shortie nightgown, climbed under the covers to watch TV.

They snapped around the channels until they found a rerun of a series they enjoyed and then dozed through the eleven o'clock news. After the weather forecast, they switched off the TV and turned out the light. As usual, they cuddled together, Liz on her right side and Kyle on his right side, pressed spoon-style against her back. He wrapped his arm around her chest and cupped her breast.

"Ummm," Liz said, halfway between being awake and asleep.

His mouth close to her ear, Kyle said, "I love the way your breast just fills my hand and your ass just fits my groin. We must be perfectly matched."

Liz suddenly became more awake. It excited her when Kyle talked to her this way and she could feel her body react.

He breathed a hot stream of air onto her ear, then whispered, "I love to make love to you. You're always so warm and so soft." He squeezed her breast, circling his fingers lightly on the flesh around her nipple. "Your nipple gets so hard when I touch you."

Kyle's breath caressed Liz's neck as he said, "When we make love, your breasts seem to swell. They feel full of all the lust you feel."

As he continued to stroke her breast, Liz, wide awake now, moved slightly to grant him easier access to her body.

"That's right," he purred, "move so I can touch you more easily. I know how much you like it when I fondle your tits. I can squeeze your nipples and feel them getting harder." His hands did exactly what he told her he was doing. "I can pinch them until they hurt."

As he rubbed her nipple between his fingers, Liz

moved her hips slightly and Kyle seized upon that movement.

"Yes, move your hips. When you move, even a little, the wet lips of your pussy rub together. You like that, don't you?"

"Ummm" was all Liz said, her breathing heavy.

"I've stroked this breast, but I haven't spent any time fondling the other one." His hand moved to Liz's other breast. "The nipple isn't hard yet." He pinched her. "But I can fix that. I can suck and tease your tits to make you get hotter and hotter between your legs."

Liz was slightly embarrassed by Kyle's comments every time she moved, but she was having a difficult time holding still. Kyle knew that, too.

"You want to move your hips, don't you? You want to rub your thighs together to scratch that itch between your legs. I'm making you hungry, aren't I?"

"Yes," Liz whispered.

"Move your hips," he said, his breath hot on her ear, his hand ceaselessly caressing her breasts. "Go ahead. When you move your hips, you rub your sweet little ass against my hard prick."

Liz held still, not wanting Kyle to know exactly how right he was.

"Come on, baby, don't resist. You know you want to." He nipped at Liz's shoulder.

She did want to feel his hard cock, so she rubbed her buttocks against Kyle's erection.

"That's the way, baby. Stroke my cock with your ass while I rub your tits." His hands were never still, first stroking with soft feather touches, then suddenly pinching Liz's increasingly sensitive nipples. When he wasn't whispering in her ear, he was licking and nipping at her neck and shoulder.

"I'll bet your pussy is all wet. I'll bet your clit is swollen and hard, just like a tiny cock waiting for me to touch it." He bit her earlobe lightly.

Liz was silent. She didn't want to break the spell. Kyle was close to making her come without any vaginal contact.

"I know just what your pussy feels like," Kyle continued. "It's hot and wet, needing to be touched. Do you want me to touch your pussy? You want me to slide my fingers between your legs and rub your clit." When she was silent, he said, "Tell me how much you want me."

"Oh, yes. I want you so much," Liz said, her voice breathy and her breathing quick.

"Say please."

"Please," Liz murmured.

"No. Not quite yet," Kyle said. "I won't touch you just yet." He loved the power his words had over Liz. She was reacting as if he was fucking her, although he was only touching her breasts. He wondered whether he could actually make her come without any vaginal contact.

"I'll bet I could make you come without even touching you," he murmured. "I'll bet you're hot enough right now to come with only the slightest push." He established a rhythm, kneading Liz's breast and pulling at her nipple. "Of course, I could touch you. I could rub my slippery finger over your clit. I could run my finger over the length of it, then brush my fingertip over the sensitive part at the end.

"Then maybe I'd slip one finger deep into your sweet, hot pussy. I'd slide it in very deep, then pull it all the way out."

Kyle could feel Liz's hips moving rhythmically against his belly and cock in the same rhythm with which he was kneading her breast. It had become almost a game. Could he get her to climax? His pajama-covered erection nestled between her bare cheeks. Even through the cloth, her heat astounded him.

"You want it so much," he continued. "You want my fingers inside you, first one, then two. Maybe I'll spread you wide open and press three fingers deep into your pussy. First, I'll push them all the way in, then pull them out and brush them over your clit. Then I'll push them back inside you. First in deep, then out and over your clit. Then in deep again, then out."

He fucked her with his voice. Her hips were bucking against his cock as her thighs rubbed together. He felt her hand move. "I know what you want to do. You want to touch yourself so you can come. You want to reach between your legs and rub that magic spot that makes you come. But I don't want you to. Put both your hands up here on my arm."

Liz moved her hands up and placed them on the arm that was still wrapped around her.

"You want to come, don't you?"

"Oh yes," she answered.

"How does it feel when you come? Does it wash over you in waves?"

Liz was losing control of her body. Waves of heat coursed through her.

"Do the muscles of your pussy spasm?" As he said the word *spasm,* he suddenly pinched her nipple, hard. "Come for me. Come right now."

Liz felt her body start to climax. "Oh God, yes," she cried. "It's so good. Fuck me now!"

He wanted to be inside of her while she was still climaxing. Kyle shifted his position only slightly, pulled down his pajama pants, and quickly slid his hard cock deep into her pussy from behind. Her contractions on his cock were too much. It took only a few thrusts until he came.

Later, Liz said, "Wow! I didn't know that was possible." She paused, then said sleepily, "I came without you even touching my cunt."

"It's never been any better for me, either," Kyle said into the darkness. He laughed. "Someone once said that one picture is worth a thousand words. I'd argue that he just didn't know the right words."

Sometimes the words may be used not during lovemaking but before, to tantalize and pleasantly frustrate. And it's not just the one hearing the words who gets the pleasure.

CARL'S STORY

Carl sat behind his traditional maple desk and stared out the window of his large corner office. The morning had been tedious, filled with long, boring meetings and three useless phone calls. He had spent a long lunch wining and dining a prospective client and now, having had a bit too much to drink, he was slightly tipsy.

He picked up a financial report and tried to concentrate on its contents. It didn't work. His alcohol-relaxed mind kept straying to his wife, Maria. She was due home that night from a two-week business trip, and he had missed both her company and her luscious body. It was their first long separation after almost two years of marriage.

Idly, he reached a heavy hand down to the front of his slacks. He was already erect as he remembered all the times they had made love together. How many more hours?

The intercom buzzed. He pressed the button and said, "Yes?"

"Your wife is on line three," his secretary's disembodied voice said.

He smiled and punched the appropriate button on the phone.

"I hope you're not calling to say you'll be delayed," he said without preamble.

"And hello to you, too," Maria said with a slight chuckle in her voice.

"Sorry. I was just thinking about us. It makes me impatient."

"That's good. I'm impatient, too."

"Where are you?" Carl asked.

"I'm at the airport, waiting for my flight home. I've got a half an hour to kill, so I thought I'd call."

They chatted for a few moments and exchanged news that had come up since their conversation late the previous evening.

"You said you were thinking about us when I called," Maria said when the conversation lagged.

Carl shifted the phone to his other ear and settled more comfortably into his oversized desk chair. "I was just thinking about the last time we made love."

He could hear her long sigh from the other end of the phone. He smiled as he thought of her long, shapely legs, her tiny breasts, and blond pubic mound. "Are there a lot of people around you?" he asked.

She was puzzled at the sudden change of topic. "I'm standing in the middle of the waiting area and there are hundreds of people bustling from somewhere to somewhere else. Why do you ask?"

"Because I think I'll tell you in detail some things I want you to do before you get home. I may also tell you all about how our lovemaking is going to be tonight."

"You're the boss, of course," Maria said. Early in their relationship, they had discovered their mutual enjoyment of Carl taking the dominant role and Maria the completely submissive one, and they had refined it over the last year. "But, darling," she protested, "I'm out here in the middle of all these people. If you get me as hot as your talking usually does, what am I supposed to do with my hunger?"

"That's not my concern, is it?" Carl heard a shuddering sigh. Then he heard his wife's husky voice. "You're a devil, darling," she whispered, "but what choice do I have. I'm listening."

"Do you have your trench coat with you?" Carl asked.

Maria looked over at her black trench coat draped over one of the chairs. "It's here."

"Good. Before you arrive, I want you to go into the bathroom on the plane and take off everything you're wearing except your garter belt, stockings, and shoes. Put your clothes in your briefcase, then put the trench coat on."

"Carl, you're kidding. I can't do that."

"Are you arguing with me, darling?" His voice was mild but firm.

Maria hesitated. She pictured herself wearing the coat, closed and belted. Yes, she thought, I could arrange it so that no one would notice. She felt herself getting wet at the thought. "No, darling. I'm not arguing."

"Good. While you're in the bathroom changing, if you're very excited, you have my permission to masturbate and come. Once only. I want you hot but not too excited when you arrive. I have a long evening planned. Do you understand?"

"I do."

"Okay. I'll see you at the airport at seven-ten."

"Good-bye, darling," Maria said, her eyes on her trench coat. She could already feel her naked nipples rub against the silky lining of the coat. Knees shaking, she picked up her things and walked toward the gate.

Carl hung up the phone and closed his eyes. He could picture his wife coming toward him at the airport. Yes, he thought, only he would know what she was, or wasn't, wearing. He glanced at his watch. There were only three and a half hours to wait—not too long to wait for an evening like the one he was planning.

It is obvious from the story that Carl and Maria have learned one lesson that is worth stressing. The fun of a sexual encounter should begin with the first thought. Anticipation can play an integral part in any sex game. You can call your partner and tell him what to look forward to that evening. Or you can tie a ribbon around your partner's wrist so that anytime he looks at it he'll know you have special plans.

Here's a sexy idea. Buy some new underwear, a teddy or sexy lace panties from a catalog. Cut out the catalog picture. The evening that you first wear your new undies, dress in secret so that only you know what you're wearing underneath your clothes. As you leave the house, hand your partner the picture. Tell him that you're wearing some new "gift wrap" and he can see it later when you get home. Guys, you can do the same thing with new satin briefs or tiny shorts in a bright color. Need I say more?

Whispering erotica, as Kyle did with Liz, and using words to titillate the mind, as Carl did for Maria, are wonderful ways to use sound to excite your partner. But storytelling can have a much more serious purpose. It can allow you to discuss sexual topics that are still too difficult to talk about freely.

Storytelling allows you to venture into any area of sexual experimentation that you want and test the waters. You know the signs that indicate your partner is excited by what you are saying. You've learned these signals over the years of your relationship. Those signs can tell you that some activity you thought would be taboo is really all right with your partner. If you get no response, you can try again another time.

The other aspect of storytelling is story listening. If your partner is telling you a story, listen for hidden messages. If you hear something that suggests an off-center activity that you've never tried, use body language, or say, "Sounds exciting," to transmit an "I'm interested" message. Then, if necessary, ask your partner about it later. The encouraging phrase "Would you really like to try..." said with a grin both excites and initiates communication. Be aware that the answer to such a question may range from silence to a tiny nod. Your partner may mention things in a story that he might ordinarily be too inhibited to suggest.

When you venture into new territory, you may want to begin slowly. To use a sense of taste analogy, if all you've done with your partner so far is plain vanilla sex or maybe a bit of vanilla fudge or coffee, you probably want to move to chocolate chip, then to Oreos and Cream. It may take a while to reach Heavenly Hash, but you'll taste so many wonderful things along the way.

How can you begin such a dialogue?

First, select a story from any chapter in this book, one that excites you. Then, the next time you are both relaxed and in the mood for loving, read it aloud. Even if you think it's the furthest thing from your partner's desires, try anyway. Wouldn't it be a wonderful surprise to discover that your partner is interested in the same activity you are? In other words, use the story to mention some sexual experiment that you've always wanted to try and see what his or her reaction is.

If your partner seems to be excited by what you suggest, the next step is to try it, maybe right after the end of the storytelling. If you can't find a story in here that says what you want to say, make one up. However you do it, storytelling is a wonderful way to suggest a new activity. If an activity is suggested during storytelling, don't prejudge. Remember, no activity is bad if it is done between two consenting adults.

Some hints about trying something new: If, while you're listening to a story that your partner's telling, you find that the story is venturing into an area you don't like, take over the plot and direct it differently. When your partner pauses for breath, interrupt and say, "Or maybe..." That sends a clear signal that this isn't your thing but also suggests an alternative.

Be sure that you watch for all the signals as you progress. An idea might have been fun to listen to but not fun to try. Remember also that when trying something new, you must reinforce positive feelings. Purr when something feels good or say, "That feels wonderful" or "Do that again."

It is just as important, however, that you delicately express any negative feelings. It doesn't improve your lovemaking if you're enduring something for the sake of your partner. You will resent it and your partner will soon discover that something's wrong. Don't suffer in silence. Say, "That idea wasn't my thing" or "Could we do it this way instead."

If you are expressing negative feelings, be sure that you reinforce that it's the activity you didn't like, not your partner. If you handle the situation with care, you can try all kinds of things with relatively little risk and probably discover many that you both enjoy.

At first, telling stories in bed can be embarrassing and awkward. Where do you start? Anywhere you want. Use one of the stories in this book as a jumping-off place.

For those of you who don't respond to any of these stories, I've created what I call story starters, several of which I've included below. In them, I set the scene and introduce the players. Then I stop the story, just when things start heating up. That's where you take over.

One note: In my stories, and most others I read, all the characters are handsome, beautiful people, physically perfect in every way. Most of us can't even come close to resembling the paragons of perfection we read about. That's fine. Use your imagination. Think beautiful, handsome thoughts about your partner and about yourself. Flow with them. That in itself enhances your lovemaking.

RECOLLECTION

Ruth bent over to pick up a box of laundry detergent. As she lifted the heavy box into her shopping cart, she caught a quick glimpse of the tall man just rounding the corner into the next aisle.

"It can't be," she muttered. "Nah."

She continued her shopping, occasionally glancing at the man as he roamed the supermarket ahead of her. Each time she saw him, she was sure he looked familiar, but it couldn't be.

She arrived at the front of the store and groaned. As usual, the lines were long. "Summer people," she muttered. Things were so quiet during the winter. Once the weather got warm, however, the mobs appeared.

Resigned, knowing she was going to be standing there for at least a half an hour, she chose the shortest line and looked around. There he was, standing in the next checkout line.

Softly, she said, "Perry?"

He turned as he looked for the source of the voice. Suddenly, their eyes locked. "Ruth?"

"Perry," Ruth said, her heart pounding, "is it really you?"

"Ruth, I don't believe it. After all these years. How long has it been?"

"Since we graduated in 1978."

Perry moved his cart into the line behind Ruth. "I remember that summer so well," he said. "The beach, that fire by the ocean. Wow."

Ruth remembered every moment of their brief summer affair. Their romance had blazed as hot as the summer nights. They had made love almost constantly and had vowed they would love one another forever.

"Did college work out for you?" Ruth asked. "As I

recall, you didn't want to go all the way to California, but it was the only way you could afford to continue your education."

Geography, Perry thought. It had always been against them. Three thousand miles for a damn scholarship. "It turned out fine. I graduated, went on to law school, and I'm now practicing in Los Angeles. What about you?"

Ruth sighed. "I went for two years, then I met Stan. We got married the summer before my junior year. I never finished that year. I got pregnant. Bret is almost nine."

"You're married? That's great."

Did Ruth hear a bit of regret in his voice? "I'm divorced. It's been three years now."

The line moved forward. When Ruth was settled again, she said, "How about you? Married?"

"Nope. I guess I never found anyone as wonderful as you." Perry grinned, but the smile never made it to his eyes.

"Why didn't you write?" Ruth said quietly.

"At the time, I thought it was best to break clean." Perry hesitated. "Now I wonder."

Ruth shook her head to clear it. Even with a shopping cart between them, Perry was too close. After all these years, he still excited her.

"What brings you back here from the West Coast?"

"My mom died about a month ago and I'm here to close up and sell the house."

Ruth had always liked Perry's mother. "I'm so sorry."

"Don't be. She had been ill since my dad died. I

think she is happier now." He paused. "Listen. How about an evening out, just for old times' sake?"

"I don't know," Ruth said. "Maybe it's not such a good idea."

"I think it's a wonderful idea." Perry's voice became wistful. "We could go to that little Italian restaurant we used to love, then take a walk on the beach. It would be like that summer."

Ruth was sure that it would be. She knew herself well enough to know that if they spent time together, she wouldn't be able to resist him. She looked into Perry's eyes and saw the same thoughts. God, she remembered their passion and her body responded the way it always had.

Perry walked around his cart and stood next to her. He deliberately fastened his eyes on her nipples, swollen and projecting from the front of her T-shirt. "For old times' sake?" he whispered.

Ruth nodded. "Why not. For old times' sake."

PERFECTION

"Miss Harper," Jackie's boss said, sticking his head into her office, "I'd like you to attend the meeting with some representatives of the Pennington Corporation this afternoon so you can present some of your ideas for the new advertising campaign. They may have some changes or suggestions. Two o'clock in the conference room."

"Of course, Mr. Brock," Jackie answered. As her boss pulled back and closed her office door, Jackie groaned. She hated meetings with company bigwigs who liked to throw their weight around and change things just for the sake of changing them. Her campaign was good. She knew that.

"Oh well," she said aloud. "What choice do I have?" She sighed and glanced at her watch. "Just enough time to prepare for battle with a good lunch."

At two o'clock, she was seated at Mr. Brock's right at the conference table, waiting for the Pennington Company representatives. Fuming, she muttered, "Just like corporate executives. Keep the little folks waiting."

As she muttered, the door opened and three men walked in. Jackie saw only the first one. He was gorgeous, six foot three, dark wavy hair, piercing blue eyes, broad shoulders. Stunned by the man's good looks, Jackie barely heard Mr. Brock's introductions. "Miss Harper, I'd like you to meet Mr. Thomas Pennington and his two vice presidents."

Jackie reached out to shake the Adonis's hand. "Nice to meet you, Mr. Pennington," she murmured.

"Nice to meet you, Miss Harper," he said, holding her hand a heartbeat longer than necessary.

Mr. Brock cleared his throat and introduced Jackie to the other two men. "Shall we begin?" he said.

Jackie had no idea how she got through the presentation, but somehow it was suddenly four-thirty. Her mouth was dry, so she took a sip of water from the glass in front of her, then glanced at her easel.

She knew that she must have done the presentation, because her flip charts were all turned, but she didn't remember a word she had said.

Mr. Pennington stood up and said, "I'm very impressed with your ideas, Miss Harper, but I still have a few questions. Why don't we discuss them over a drink?"

She hesitated. She dated on a regular basis but her dates were usually with men introduced to her by friends. This man was a perfect stranger and, besides, she doubted the wisdom of mixing business with pleasure. She sighed. Perfect. Yes, she had to admit, he certainly was.

Putting her doubts aside, she agreed. "That would be fine, Mr. Pennington."

"Call me Tom," he said softly.

"All right, Tom," she replied. "My name's Jackie."

INTIMIDATION

"Who is he?" Terry asked, staring out her window at the well-built man pushing one of her father's cars across the front driveway.

"Pardon?" Grace, the maid, said as she finished making the bed.

"Nothing," Terry said. As she watched, the man pulled off his shirt and threw it into the driver's window. Then he pressed the palms of his huge hands against the hood of the car with all his strength, causing his sweat-dampened back muscles to ripple. Slowly, the car began to inch its way toward the garage.

"That's Steven, Miss Terry," the maid said, looking over Terry's shoulder. "He's the new mechanic and handyman your father just hired to care for his cars and whatever. Gorgeous, isn't he?"

"Ummm," Terry purred. "He certainly is. What do you know about him?"

"His name's Steven Brownstone and he's twenty-eight and single. He comes with good references. Used to work for someone famous—I don't remember who."

"Thanks, Grace," Terry said, continuing to stare. He has great arms and shoulders, she thought as Steven and the car stopped in front of the garage. And a great ass, too.

"You going to invite him to play?" Grace asked. She knew all about Terry's exotic tastes in men and sex and had, on occasion, joined her in one of her escapades.

"I think I just might," Terry answered.

"Can I join you? He's *so* beautiful."

"Maybe later. For the moment, I just want to try him out myself."

It was later that afternoon when Terry wandered into the garage. Steven, still shirtless, was bending over one front fender, dwarfing her father's tiny pet MG.

"I understand your name's Steven," Terry said loudly.

Steven pulled himself up and looked down at the

diminutive young woman facing him. "That's me. And you're...?"

"You shall call me Miss Terry," she said, her eyes raking his body, taking in his smooth, grease-stained torso and shoulder-length blond hair. Not really handsome, Terry thought, but rugged and strong.

Steven looked Terry over, too. She came up only to his shoulders. He noted the springy light brown curls all over her head and that she was wearing only a halter top and a pair of brief short-shorts that left just enough to the imagination. Even without makeup, she was a knockout. Steven felt himself getting aroused.

They stood examining each other for a moment, then Steven said, "Did you want something? I have work to do."

"I want something, all right, but not here and not now." With a sudden movement, she reached over and cupped his balls through his jeans. He wanted to pull away, but her gaze froze him. She slid her hand up, squeezing his hardness. "Very nice equipment you have," she said, withdrawing her hand. "Very nice, indeed. And I'll bet you think you know how to use it."

Steven was so flabbergasted that he couldn't speak.

Terry turned and walked toward the door. Over her shoulder, she said, "Tomorrow morning, nine-thirty. Meet me down at the pool."

Gathering his thoughts, Steven said, "I have a job here, you know. Tomorrow's a workday."

"Oh, you'll be working, all right. For me. Remember, nine-thirty. Sharp."

"But your father..."

"He understands me very well. That's part of the reason he hired you, part of the job requirement, if you will. If you want to keep this job, you'll have to keep me happy, not my father. Men are hired and fired around here because of what *I* want. Is that perfectly clear?"

He nodded. When he was sent here by the agency yesterday, they had warned him that the job requirements were unusual. But the job paid twice what he had been making, and if staying meant that he'd have to keep Miss Terry happy, that would be fine.

He smiled, watching Terry's firm ass as she closed the door behind her. Weird, he thought, very weird. Nine-thirty by the pool? He knew he'd be there, doing whatever she wanted.

MEDICATION

"Your wife has never had an orgasm?" the little man asked.

"No, and that's why I'm here." Brad was still amazed at his own gullibility. Here he was in a dingy store that sold POTIONS OF ALL KINDS. But his friend Rick had told him that some amazing things went on in this store, and by now, Brad was willing to try anything.

Denise: She was such a good wife and a wonderful mother. And in bed, she was always willing and eager to please. But Brad was sure she had never had an orgasm. At the end of their lovemaking, he was always satiated, and Denise would cuddle up against him and tell him of her love. But no matter how long he teased and licked and fondled, she never climaxed. He was at his wit's end.

"No orgasm," the little man muttered. "No orgasm." He hunted around under the counter. "Very common problem. You'd be amazed." As he stood up, his glasses slipped down his wrinkled nose. "Now where did I put those vials?"

He puttered around for what seemed like hours until he finally found the box he had been searching for. "Here they are," he said. He pulled a vial out of the box and handed it to Brad.

Brad looked at the golden liquid in the vial. "What do I do with this?" he asked.

"Well, it's very simple," the old man said. "It can be used on any part of the body as long as that part has been properly prepared."

"Prepared?"

"Right. First, you have to get the particular part aroused. Like breasts. You have to suck your wife's nipples until they are rock-hard and wet from your mouth. Then you spread a bit of this oil over her skin and wait. The ingredients are absorbed through the wet flesh."

"Just on her breasts?"

"Of course not. The more of the potion you can get into her system, the better. It affects the part you put it on, and the entire system. You can put it on her mouth, her breasts, her vagina, anywhere you want to heighten excitement. I guarantee she will get so hot that she will climax."

"It sounds simple enough, but how much does this magic cost?"

The little man quoted a price and Brad was amazed. "That's very reasonable."

"I'm very partial to people who want this particular potion. They want something wonderful for another person, so I try to please. One last word of advice. You should have to use the potion only for the first night. Once your wife has an orgasm, her body will remember how forever after. If you do need to use it again, however, use less the second time, then still less, until you need no more." He winked. "You can use it on yourself, as well, if you wish. It stimulates and gives pleasure to both men and women."

Brad paid the man, then left the store with the carefully wrapped vial in his pocket. As he drove home, he vacillated between excitement and disbelief.

At first, Brad wanted to try the potion immediately, but as the day progressed, he found that knowing what was to come heightened his pleasure. That evening, Brad and Denise enjoyed a good dinner. Frequently, Brad reached into his pocket to touch the vial. After dinner, the couple went to a movie, a romantic comedy with lots of suggestive sex scenes. By the time they returned home, both were in the mood for making love.

While Denise was brushing her teeth in the bathroom, Brad took the vial out of his pocket and placed it on the bedside table. Yes, he thought, that's right where I want it, within easy reach.

Brad watched as Denise came back into the bedroom and stretched out on the bed. "Darling," he said, "tonight is going to be special. Very special."

EXPECTATION

"I will not!" Sharon said, amazed that things had progressed so far. "I will not marry a man I don't even know!"

"My dear, you will do as you're told." Her father's voice was deadly quiet. "I made this arrangement with your best interests at heart. I've met the young man and he's very handsome and very rich."

"If he's so rich and handsome, what does he want from me?" Sharon looked down at her mother's ivory lace wedding dress, waiting for her, spread across the bed.

"Our family's land abuts his and it has been planned since you were born that you and he would marry. He will do his duty, just as you will."

"Nonsense! I will not!" Sharon cried. "You can't marry me off like you'd sell a horse. I'll not marry a man I've never met."

Sharon's father continued. "Darling, I think I've made it very plain. You will do as you're told or you'll be disinherited. I will ask you to leave this house and never return."

Sharon knew that her father was serious. She looked

at her mother, who had started to cry. She walked over and put her arm around the older woman's shoulders. "Daddy's not really serious, Mother, is he? He wouldn't banish me forever."

"Darling, I'm sure he is serious." She began to cry louder, then her face became pale and she started to cough. "Get my medicine," she gasped.

Sharon's father got his wife's medicine out of her pocketbook and poured her a spoonful. Sharon watched as her mother stopped coughing and her color returned to normal.

"Listen, darling," her father said. "Walt's father and I only want an heir to whom we can leave the combined resources of our land. I have Walt's assurance that once you produce an heir, you will be free to do whatever you wish."

"Father," Sharon yelled, horrified, "you discussed all that with him?"

"Of course. All you need to do is get pregnant and have a healthy baby, girl or boy, who will inherit all the lands. Then you can divorce him, as long as you understand that any further children either of you have may lay no claim to the estate. If you wish, I'll even put a considerable sum in the bank in trust for you. Then you can go off as a young divorcée and see the world, do whatever you want."

Sharon was amazed at herself. She was letting her father talk her into this nonsense.

Sensing that his daughter was wavering, Sharon's father played his trump card. "Come here, my dear," he said, walking over to the door of the dressing

room. He opened the door a crack and peered out.
Then he stepped back so Sharon could look.

"That's him," her father said.

Sharon looked out through the crack in the door.
Standing with his back to her in the hallway was a tall
man dressed in a tuxedo. He does have a beautiful
body, she had to admit, slim hips and broad shoulders. Then he turned around. He was gorgeous:
raven black hair combed carefully away from his handsome face; deep brown eyes with long dark lashes; a
sensual mouth surrounding perfect white teeth.

Sharon caught her breath. He was quite something.
His eyes caught hers. As she pulled back into the
dressing room, she saw the beautiful man wink at her
and blow her a quick kiss.

It seemed only moments later that Sharon stood in
front of the altar, Walt at her side. As the minister
droned on, Walt leaned slightly toward her and, in a
voice only she could hear, said, "You're as beautiful as
your picture."

His voice rumbled through Sharon's body and made
her shiver. She felt his fingers as his hand found hers.
He laced his fingers through hers and put his thumb
between. Suddenly, she felt him start to scratch circles in her palm.

"Tonight's going to be wonderful," he whispered
over the priest's singsong. "Maybe, by the time our
child is born, I will have convinced you to stay with
me. I've loved you from a distance for such a long
time."

Trembling, Sharon was barely aware of the rest of
the service and the party that followed. The afternoon

passed in a fog until, finally, she and Walt were alone in the room in which they would spend that night.

Walt opened a bottle of champagne and poured two glassfuls. He handed a glass to Sharon and raised his in a toast. "To tonight and the pleasures that await us."

"To tonight," Sharon whispered.

INVITATION

Norm stretched out on the queen-sized bed and idly flipped the channels of the motel's TV set. He snapped past a rerun of "Dallas," a rerun of "Magnum P.I.," and a variety show with an unfunny comedian.

"Shit," he muttered. "I hate evenings like this. Shit, shit, shit."

He stood up and paced the room. He considered going down to the bar to try to pick up some woman, but he was tired of the same lines; the same "Where are you from?" and "What's your sign?" and "Didn't I meet you in San Diego last year at the Food Manufacturers' Convention?"

Norm opened his suitcase and pulled out the birthday card his son had made for him in school. On the front, there was a picture that looked like an airplane with a broken wing. Mike had said it was a birthday cake. Inside, the teacher had helped him letter "Happy Birthd" on one line and "ay Daddy" on the next.

There was a note from Tess, his ex-wife. "Hope this will bring you a smile on your birthday."

Norm pulled his shirttails out of his slacks and unbuttoned the shirtfront. He dragged his arms out of the sleeves and reached behind his head to remove his undershirt. He caught a glimpse of himself in the full-length mirror on the back of the bathroom door.

Instinctively, he sucked in his stomach and puffed out his chest. "Not bad, for thirty-five," he said aloud. Maybe he'd gained a few extra pounds, but not too many. He reached up and ran his long slender fingers through his straight black hair.

He walked back to the suitcase and carefully extracted a clean shirt. As he unfolded it, he thought about going downstairs for just one drink. He jumped as he heard a knock at the door.

He lifted one eyebrow. Who in the world? he wondered. He opened the door and his breath caught in his throat.

Standing in the hall was a spectacularly beautiful young woman. She had large, round, and almost black eyes, high cheekbones, and ivory skin. Her long black hair fell in gleaming waves to her waist. She wore a flowing white evening gown, elbow-length white gloves, and silver shoes. He blinked unbelievingly. It was as though she had stepped out of his favorite fantasy.

"Yes?" he said, clearing his throat.

"Are you Norman?" Her voice was soft and her lips moved sensuously as she formed the words.

"Yes." His voice was barely above a whisper.

She opened her tiny silver pocketbook and withdrew a note. "This will explain."

As Norm opened the note, the girl said, "May I come in out of the hallway?"

"Of course," he stammered. "I'm sorry." He stood aside so the girl could enter. Gracefully, she crossed the room and sat demurely on the chair in front of the desk.

For a moment, he just gazed at her and wondered whether there was any way he could get her to stay and have a drink with him.

He shook himself out of his pointless reverie and looked at the door, which was still open.

"It's all right," she said. "My reputation can take it." Her laugh was warm and came from deep in her throat.

Norm closed the door, still staring at her.

"Why don't you read the note," she suggested.

Reminded of the piece of paper in his hand, he opened and read it.

"Dear Norm," it said. "You know that I understand you better than you understand yourself, sometimes. I hope you will use my birthday present to make yourself supremely happy. Let go and live."

The note was signed, "Tess."

He looked at the girl, sitting so quietly in the small chair. "I guess you have a present for me," he said, not totally understanding. What could his ex-wife have gotten him? He knew that she had a way of knowing just the right thing, and he was curious.

Sensuously, the girl unwound her long legs and stood up. "Yes, I do," she said.

She reached behind her and in one motion unzipped her dress and let it slide to the floor. She wore a tiny white teddy underneath, with long garters and white stockings. Her skin was alabaster white, her breasts small and flat, but her nipples were large and the areolas around them almost black. They clearly showed through the fabric. Below her flat stomach, Norm could see the shadow of her dark pubic hair.

"After the woman on the phone dictated that note, she said I should tell you this. 'If you do half of the things to Toni that you used to do to me, she'll remember you fondly, always.' I'm Toni." The girl smiled. "Ever since that phone call, I've been looking forward to this evening. I've been wondering what things you two did together."

Norm hesitated just a moment. Then a smile crept across his face. He took the few steps necessary to cross the room and shook his head. "I'll never understand how Tess knows me so well, but she does. And, Toni, if you're really curious about the things that she and I did together, I'll show you."

The story starter that follows is a bit longer than most. It sets a scene and tells you quite a lot about the characters. If you're looking for a situation in which the man has all the power, it might be just the thing.

INCARCERATION

Once upon a time long ago, there was a very beautiful young lady named MaryClaire. Her father, a rich and powerful Spanish landowner, searched all over Spain for a proper husband for his daughter because she was already eighteen and getting too old for a good match. When he found no one quite right, he sent men all over the world to find a gentleman who was rich, powerful, and not too old. He finally chose the Spanish governor of a small island in the Caribbean. The man was very wealthy and owned a huge plantation and several ships that traded spices around the world. It was said that he wasn't too bad-looking and he was only fifty-one.

Without much warning, MaryClaire and her chaperone were packed up and shipped off to the New World on a sleek schooner, protected by two dozen handpicked soldiers. Protection, of course, was vital on the high seas.

The ship was only a week from its destination when pirates attacked. Since her chaperone had been trapped in the galley by the fighting, MaryClaire was alone in the spacious cabin at the front of the ship. The fighting was fierce and MaryClaire could hear the clashing of swords and the cries of men. If the pirates won the battle, what would happen to her?

Her eyes darted about the room until she spotted a large trunk that had held the linens that were now on the bed. Quickly, MaryClaire lifted the heavy top and climbed inside. She curled up and slowly lowered the lid. She hadn't considered what she would do when she was forced to come out.

MaryClaire spent what seemed like hours cramped inside the trunk before the sounds of fighting subsided. Moments later, she heard heavy footsteps and a crash as the door to her cabin flew open. Loud voices and laughing seeped through to her ears as men searched the room. And there was nothing she could do but pray that no one would lift the lid of the trunk and expose her hiding place.

There was a scraping sound and then laughter. "Look at this, Captain," one male voice said. "There must be a king's ransom in jewels here."

Maybe they'll be so happy about finding my jewels that they'll leave, she prayed. But it was not to be.

"Search the room," another voice ordered. "There must be someone around here who wears these baubles. It can't be that old crone we found in the galley."

There were other sounds, then the lid of the trunk was jerked open. A hand grabbed MaryClaire's arm, pulled her up, and held her small, supple body aloft by her wrist.

"Captain," the man said, "look what I found."

With powerful strides, a man who was obviously the pirate captain crossed the room. As MaryClaire looked at him, she was momentarily impressed by his tall, muscular body and handsome face. His hair was dark, as was his full, closely cropped beard, and his eyes were the palest blue, like pieces of summer sky that shined from his deeply tanned skin. She almost smiled until she remembered that this handsome man was a ruthless pirate. She closed her eyes tightly and fought to free herself, unwittingly displaying her voluptuous body.

"Very nice, Billy," the captain said, nodding in appreciation. "Very nice, indeed. I think I'll keep her for the moment." He pulled a sheet off the bed and wrapped the wriggling MaryClaire in it. "There's no need to let the men see her, and you're not to tell anyone about her. I want no jealousy or hostility." Then he tossed the girl over the mate's shoulders. "Take her across to my ship and put her in my cabin. I'll get to her later. If she's worth the effort, I'll compensate the men with my share of the treasure."

He slapped MaryClaire across the behind and growled. "Make a sound or struggle and I'll change my plans and give you to my men and keep the treasure. Do you understand what that means?"

MaryClaire's reluctant "Yes" was muffled by the layers of sheeting around her.

MaryClaire remembered very little of her trip to the pirate ship. When she arrived in the captain's cabin, the pirate who was carrying her unwrapped the sheet, dumped her on the captain's bed, and locked her in. He returned moments later with a long rope and used one end of it to tie her wrists together. Then he tied the other end to the thick wooden bedpost. He gazed at her heaving chest for a moment, sighed, turned, and loudly locked the door behind him as he left.

MaryClaire looked around the cabin. It was well furnished and had a few valuable paintings on the wall and silver candlesticks everywhere. There was an Oriental carpet on the floor and rich silks on the bed. This must be a man of some taste, she thought, so maybe I can bargain with him. Maybe he'll be interested in the ransom my father would pay to get me back unharmed.

She waited for a long time for the captain to arrive. The sun set and, in the darkness, when she could no longer stay awake, she fell into an exhausted sleep.

It was many hours later when the pirate captain finally walked into the room, holding a candle. He looked at the bed and at the beautiful girl his first mate had pulled from the trunk. He had been looking forward to this moment all day, but his duties had forced him to put off this meeting until now.

He studied the girl as the candlelight illuminated the long black hair that was spread over her face and shoulders. Long dark lashes lay across her creamy white cheeks. Her mouth was soft and the captain longed to possess it, but this girl was a rare treasure and he knew he had lots of time. His gaze ranged lower. Her dress had ripped during her struggles and now he could see the tops of her full breasts. Her waist was tiny and one bare foot and well-formed ankle peeked out from under her skirt.

He rubbed the bulge in the front of his pants. Patience, he told himself, we have a long time.

The girl stirred, her eyes opened, and she saw the captain. She sat up and said, "My father will pay a great deal to get me back unharmed."

"That's not at all what I had in mind. Remember, I turned down my share of the treasure that was carried aboard your ship in order to have you." A smile curved the corners of his mouth.

"You can't mean to harm me." MaryClaire sounded more confident than she felt.

"You must understand some basics." The captain sat down in a chair and put his feet up on the desk next to the bed. Thick thigh muscles rippled under his tight pants and curls of black hair showed above his partly buttoned shirt. "You are here because I find you very beautiful." He leaned over and ran his index finger over her cheek. MaryClaire tried not to react to the sensuous touch of his hand.

"If you were ugly," he continued, "I would have given you to my men. We've been at sea for a long time and they could use some diversion. If you don't please me, I may do that, anyway."

MaryClaire stared silently at the captain.

"You are the only one here from your ship, so there's no one to help or rescue you."

She shuddered. "What happened to the men and Isabel, my chaperone?"

"Don't worry. My crew and I are very good at what we do and we seldom find it necessary to kill anyone. Fortunately, during the struggle, none of your men were even seriously injured. We left them all on your ship, along with that old crow whom we found in the galley. After unloading the treasure, we disabled the ship so it couldn't follow us, but we left them plenty of food and water. They will reach land eventually, but unfortunately for you, it won't be soon enough to do you any good."

She closed her eyes to try to blot out the things the captain was saying and calm her racing heart, but it did no good. He just kept talking and her heart continued to pound.

"Are you hungry?"

She slowly opened her eyes. "Yes," she managed to say.

"Well, you must learn a few truths. The first is that you'll eat when I'm pleased with you."

She drew a breath to protest but then stopped. There was no point in resisting, because there was no way out.

He saw the resignation settle across her face. "Good. I can see you're beginning to understand your position. You have no choices." His smile showed even white teeth.

MaryClaire shivered from both fear and expectation.

"You really shouldn't be frightened," he said calmly. "Many women have found themselves in a similar predicament and have made the best of things. I think you're a smart girl. Now, come over here. I won't hurt you." His voice became a warm purr. "As a matter of fact, I will show you pleasures such as you've never known."

She took a deep breath, straightened her shoulders, and crawled to the edge of the bed. He's handsome, she thought, and I would like to just drown myself in his eyes. But I'm a lady and I have my pride. She stood up, stretching the rope tightly. She held the remains of her torn dress in front of her.

"Drop your arms. I want to see what I've gone to so much trouble to acquire." He said everything with complete calm. He was in total control and he knew it. So did MaryClaire.

Slowly, she dropped her arms. Her torn dress fell to her waist, exposing the tops of her breasts. Calmly, the pirate captain reached out and yanked at the front of her camisole. The fabric ripped down to her waist and her full breasts spilled out.

He saw the soft flesh and large dark brown nipples. He expected the girl to cower but she held her head up and looked him in the eye as her chest heaved and her breasts moved excitingly in front of his face.

"Come closer," he said huskily.

She held up her tethered wrists. "That's a little difficult," she said.

"If I untie you, will you promise not to try anything?"

"Is there anything I can do that might result in my freedom?"

"Nothing," he said.

She sighed and her shoulders drooped. "Then there's really no point in my fighting you, is there?" she said, her voice a whisper.

"None," he said. He pulled a knife out of the top of his boot and cut the rope that bound her wrists. Then he quickly cut off the rest of her clothes so she stood naked in front of him.

His eyes roamed her body. "Very nice," he said. "Very nice, indeed."

MaryClaire stared at the floor to avoid the piercing sky blue eyes that were inspecting every inch of her. No one had ever looked at her naked body and she was dreadfully embarrassed. She was surprised, though, that she was not really afraid. Totally unexpected feelings swept over her body as she raised her gaze and looked into the captain's eyes.

When he chuckled, she snapped back to reality and tried to cover herself with her hands.

"Don't do that," he snapped. "I like looking at you." He looked into her large dark eyes. "What's your name, girl?"

"MaryClaire," she murmured.

"Well, MaryClaire, we have all the time in the world before we move on to other pleasures." His emphasis on the last word made her tremble. "But I'm not here to torture you. You said you were hungry. Let's have some dinner first."

The captain walked out of the cabin and returned a moment later, followed by a man carrying a tray. She recognized the man as the one who had pulled her out of the trunk. She grabbed a cover off of the bed and pulled it around her.

"Don't do that," the pirate barked. "I want Billy to see you and know that you are mine. I also want you to understand your predicament. You have no choices."

She stood perfectly still and clutched the blanket, unable to believe that he wanted her to display her nakedness in front of the first mate.

"I don't like to say things twice." There was an angry edge to his voice. The captain walked over to MaryClaire and pulled the blanket from her hands. Then he pushed her in front of him, grabbed her elbows, and pinned her arms behind her.

"Now, Billy," the captain said. "Notice her long legs and her beautiful breasts." Still holding her arms behind her with one hand, the captain slipped his other hand under one breast and displayed it for Billy. As much as MaryClaire struggled, she couldn't free herself from the captain's grip.

Billy's eyes raked her skin and his breathing quickened.

"I just wanted MaryClaire to understand what's in

store for her if she doesn't cooperate," the captain said. "You would like her, wouldn't you, Billy?"

Billy's eyes traveled slowly from her breasts to her thighs and then back again. "If you don't want her, Captain, don't give her to the men too quickly. Give me an hour with her first. Just one hour."

"If I tire of her, you can be the first. But we'll be in port in a few days and I'm sure Marguerite will be waiting for you."

Silently, Billy put the tray down and left.

"Now you understand, don't you?" the captain said as he released her arms.

"Yes, Captain."

He turned her around and held her by her shoulders. "If you want to eat, kiss me."

She reached up and pressed her tightly closed lips briefly against his. She had never kissed a man before and she wasn't sure how it was done.

He laughed. "Virgin kisses. What a bore. Let me give you your first lesson in how to please me." He wrapped his arms around her and crushed her against him. His tongue forced her lips open and he tasted the inside of her mouth. His hands stroked her naked back and squeezed her buttocks.

"You feel so good," he murmured.

She surrendered herself to his fiery kiss. She could hear his whispers and feel the rumble in his chest. She could feel the fabric of his shirt against her naked skin. Her body trembled and all thought of food fled. New sensations flooded her and she wanted more. She pressed her body against his and felt his rock-hard thighs through his pants.

He swept her up and placed her on the bed. Then he touched her skin. His fingers danced feathery caresses across her ribs and belly, finally allowing his hungry hands to touch her breasts. It was obvious that no one had ever touched her before, but it was also evident that she was enjoying what he was doing.

He sat back as she asked, "What are you going to do now?"

"We'll see, my dear, we'll see."

4

IF IT SMELLS SUPERB...

I stood in front of my mirror this morning finishing my morning ritual and I was suddenly struck by the lengths to which I go each day to satisfy my sense of smell. First, I shower to remove any unpleasant odors, then I use deodorant to assure that no odors return. I brush my teeth and use mouthwash to assure that my breath doesn't offend. The soap I use has a pleasant and not very long-lasting scent and my shampoo is manufactured to have a nice light fragrance. I use moisturizer and makeup with as little aroma as possible to avoid conflicts with other scents. Then I put on perfume so I smell the way I choose. I vary my perfume according to my mood. Wow.

For me, nothing turns off a good sexy mood more than the smell of an unclean body. I don't mean the smell of sweat and sex that has been generated by the evening's activities. I mean the smell of a body that hasn't bathed recently. Sometimes, if I'm not sure that I smell as sweet as I'd like, I suggest that my partner and I take a long bath together. I scent the water and we soak and wash each other. It is very stimulating and also keeps me from wondering whether he'll be turned off by my body odor. Showers work, too, but don't leave as much time as I like to touch and smell and lick and cavort.

There are particularly offensive odors. I remember an evening spent with a man who smoked. I had given up cigarettes twenty years earlier and I found the smell of stale smoke overwhelming. His breath and his clothes, even his hands as he touched me, reeked. When both partners smoke, it isn't as noticeable, but once one partner quits, the smell of cigarette smoke becomes offensive to that person. If you smoke and you're contemplating a relationship with someone who is a nonsmoker, be sure to use breath mints or gum or, better still, quit.

Your breath also says a lot about you. Don't eat garlic or onions before an evening of sex play unless you both indulge. And there are other food odors that can have adverse affects on your partner. I have a friend who hates licorice and another who detests green pepper. Both say that they can smell it on another person's breath. Be alert. If your partner hates a particular food, the smell of it on you may impede your progress.

If you cook certain foods, the smell lingers in the air long after the cleanup. After a little time exposed to the smell, you may no longer be aware of it, but someone coming into the house will know that you had shrimp or fish for dinner. A well-chosen air-freshener spray can solve that problem quickly.

Once you've eliminated the unpleasant odors, create pleasant ones. When you're considering lovemaking, use perfume, cologne, or shaving lotion. Try using a new scent, even if you have to borrow one from a friend. Be sure the sheets on the bed—if that's where you intend to make love—are clean and fresh. Create a new atmosphere by changing your brand of laundry soap or fabric softener. Sprinkle scented body powder on the bed both to please the nose and change the feel of the playground.

Flowers have traditionally been part of courtship and romance. Buy some, but smell them first. Tragically, many of the flowers we love have been so inbred that they no longer have any scent, although they are still beautiful. Try to purchase a bouquet that has some scent or pick some lilacs or roses from your own or a friend's garden. Then make love in the garden that you have created.

You can make the air in the living room or bedroom smell quite different from the way it usually does by burning a scented candle. Both the smell and the glow from the candle are particularly conducive to romantic evenings. Or try incense. It comes in many varieties, from exotic musk to sweetly floral. But be careful to place anything that is burning away from any potential fire hazard such as blowing curtains or the swaying branches of a houseplant. And be sure to blow out the candles before you fall asleep in order to avoid pools of wax on the furniture.

Try not to mix several different smells. If you do, it can make your room smell like a cheap ladies' room where they use heavy perfume to cover unpleasant odors. Or two fragrances can clash and end up offending your nose. On the other hand, if your fantasy is to make love to a stranger in a public rest room, go for it.

I read historical romance novels. Occasionally, the hero makes love to the heroine in a darkened room, thinking she is someone else. I think that's impossible. The smell of a woman's hair and skin is as individual as her walk, the shape of her face, or her voice. You can make use of that fact. An erotic experience can be sparked by completely changing your scent—not just your perfume but your shampoo, your face lotion, and your soap. Change your scent and you can change a lot about your attitude...as Ellen found out.

ELLEN'S STORY

Thirty-five-year-old Ellen had been married to Bob for more than ten years. Their three children and a part-time job kept her busy for what seemed like more hours than there were in each day. Her sexual encounters with Bob tended to be routine. Bob made all the decisions. Often Ellen wished that she could lead, tell Bob exactly what she wanted, but she never had the courage to suggest it.

For her thirty-fifth birthday, three days before, Bob had gotten her a gift set of perfume, dusting powder, and soap. It was an exotic Eastern scent, very different from the florals that she usually used. That Sunday morning, Ellen towel-dried her short hair and dusted herself with the powder. She wanted Bob to be sure she appreciated his gift. By the time she finished in the shower, the bathroom smelled like an Eastern harem. She put on a terry-cloth robe and walked into the bedroom.

Bob was stretched out on the bed in his pajama pants, reading the Sunday paper. "Wow, you smell great," he said, sitting up. "It's sort of like you are someone else." Bob closed his eyes. "It is *very* unusual." He reached for her and kissed her deeply. "Ummm, I like it," he whispered.

Different, she thought. I feel different, like I'm a whole new person. I wonder... She dropped the tone of her voice a few notes. "I'd like to be different," she said.

Bob's hands rubbed the front of his wife's shoulders. "I like you any way you are."

Ellen wrapped her hands around Bob's wrists and pushed him onto his back on the bed. "Any way I am?" she said, a gleam in her eye.

Silently, Bob opened his eyes and looked at Ellen.

"What if I was really different?" she pressed.

Bob saw a look in his wife's eyes that he had never seen before. There was a challenge in her expression that he found very exciting. He could feel himself suddenly getting aroused. "Well, the children aren't around right now. What do you have in mind?"

Ellen smiled. "Don't ask questions," she said, "and don't move." She left him lying on the bed.

She locked the bedroom door against unexpected intrusions, then rummaged around in one of her bureau drawers and retrieved a few old stockings. With her back to Bob, Ellen was still unsure of how far she could carry this new personality. When she turned back to the bed with the stockings dangling from her hand, the tent formed by the crotch of Bob's pajama pants told her all she needed to know.

"There are kingdoms in the deserts of the Far East, I'm told," she said, her voice almost purring, "where women are the masters. Women keep harems of slave men." As she slid the stockings through her hands, she saw that Bob's eyes never left them.

Ellen sat down on the edge of the bed and took Bob's wrist in her firm grip. At any sign of resistance, she would have abandoned the whole idea, but she felt none. And she was terribly aroused.

With one swift motion, she wrapped one of the stockings around Bob's wrist and tied it to the headboard so it dangled above his head. Without hesitating, she walked around the bed and tied his other wrist in the same manner. Then she studied her husband, testing his reaction.

His breathing was rapid and his legs wouldn't keep still. This must be exciting him as much as it excites me, she realized. She debated tying his ankles, but she didn't know exactly how to carry that off. Instead, she climbed on the bed and sat astride Bob's thighs, imprisoning his pajama-clad knees under her.

"Now," she said, "you're mine. And I can do whatever I want." She leaned forward and kissed Bob's mouth. Bob was unable to use his hands or arms to embrace her as he usually did. For the first time, she was in control of the depth and pressure of the kiss. She played. She kissed him softly, flicking her tongue over his lips, then deepened the kiss and used her tongue to probe his mouth.

She ran her tongue over Bob's eyelids and used the tip to tickle the inside of his ear. For ten minutes, she kissed him in all the ways she had read about in the sexy novels she devoured. Once, he started to say something, but she silenced him with her lips.

Finally, she wanted more. She waited for him to do the usual things to signal that he was ready to fondle her breasts, then suddenly realized that he wasn't in charge. She was. And his hands were tied and use-less. She sat up and stared at Bob's closed eyes. "Look at me," she snapped. His eyes flew open and he looked into Ellen's eyes.

"I want more," she said, opening the front of her robe. Her rosy nipples stood out from her small breasts. She stroked and pinched herself, something she had never done with her husband watching. His eyes never left her fingers. "I want you to suck my tits."

She leaned over and placed one nipple in his mouth. His lips encircled her areola and he drew her flesh into his mouth. "Harder," she said. He sucked, pulsing and pulling at her swollen nub.

She pulled back and changed position. "Now the other." She leaned down and Bob quickly began to suck on her other nipple. As he sucked, Ellen pulled his head harder against her. "Yes," she said, "that's very good."

As she started to rub her vagina against his hard

thighs, she felt his pajama pants in her way. She got up and yanked his pajama bottoms off. She stared momentarily at his hard cock and knew that it was hers for the taking. Not yet, she decided. Not just yet.

As she pulled off her robe, she inhaled the exotic perfume. She looked down and asked, "You like my new perfume? Don't talk, just nod."

Bob nodded.

Ellen again straddled Bob's thighs, now able to rub her slippery juices on his skin. As she rubbed her wet cunt lips over his thighs, she felt his body reach for her. She knew that he wanted to slide his cock inside of her but, with his hands tied, couldn't do anything about it.

"I want—" he said, but she interrupted.

"I don't care what you want. Be silent."

Bob closed his mouth.

Ellen closed her eyes and, using her hands to massage her breasts, continued to rub her cunt over Bob's thighs. Soon, however, his huge erection began to tempt her.

She ran her fingertips lightly over his swollen cock, then stroked and tickled his balls. "You want this inside of me, don't you?"

Bob nodded again.

"But you can't do anything about it, can you?"

Bob shook his head.

"But I can." Ellen raised her body and impaled herself on Bob's cock. "Don't you dare come yet," she said. "I need your hard prick to please me."

Bob tried to clear his mind to calm the spasms that

threatened to seize control of his body. I mustn't come, he thought. Ellen wouldn't like it.

She used a levering motion to slide his cock in and out of her wet pussy, then reached down and touched her clit. While she pleased herself, she watched her husband's face. She watched the sweat form on his brow as he tried not to come. It won't be much longer for either of us, she thought.

Then she felt the swirling. "Oh, yes," she cried. "I'm going to come now."

As she climaxed, Bob relaxed and allowed himself to come, as well. His hips bucked with hers, but Ellen still controlled the rhythm. "Oh, God, so good," she said as she collapsed across Bob's chest.

Later, Ellen untied Bob's hands and kissed the light marks on his wrists. "I would ask if what I did was okay," she purred, "but I think the answer is obvious."

"It was sensational," Bob said. "I never imagined that letting you take control would be so thrilling."

"*Letting* me take control? You had no choice. And in the future, when I want to be in control, I will."

Bob nuzzled Ellen's neck and smelled her new scent. "Yes, I suppose you will."

There are people who are turned on by the smell of leather or latex. Some people call such behavior *fetishism,* a word filled with negative connotations. I must repeat the tenet upon which this book is based: *Anything that excites and doesn't hurt anyone is okay.* All kinds of games are possible and there are as many things that excite as there are people.

Sandy, for example, had always been turned on by

the smell of leather, but it wasn't until she found a way to let her husband, Paul, know that that the fun began.

SANDY'S STORY

Sandy loved leather. She loved the feel of it and the look of it, but mostly she loved the smell of it. It may have originally had something to do with her first boyfriend, a biker type who always dressed in a black leather jacket, chaps, and leather gloves. They had gone together for over a year, traveling around on his motorcycle. But, after they graduated from high school, they went their separate ways, leaving Sandy with a special feeling about leather.

She owned her own leather jacket and wore it frequently, but it wasn't the same as being held by someone who smelled of that wonderful animal smell. Once in a while, Sandy visited the mall and spent some time in a leather-clothing store. Once she tried on a leather miniskirt in a room in the back of the store. Because she wore a size sixteen, she thought the skirt looked awful, but the feel of it against her skin was a turn-on.

In contrast to her biker, Sandy's husband, Paul, was an accountant. They had met when she went to work as his secretary, dated for a few months, and then married. Now, almost five years later, they were still as much in love as they had been when they'd first met. As their initial passion wore off, it was replaced by a varied sex life that included many off-center sex games. They trusted each other and communicated most of their fantasies—but not Sandy's love of leather.

Sandy was convinced that her leather fetish was too weird to mention to Paul. Granted, six months ago, he had confessed that he wanted to try anal sex and that had developed into an exciting addition to their sex play. But Sandy thought that leather was just too kinky.

Then she came across a book. Although she had read many sex articles that said fetishes were okay, they had failed to impress her the way that book did. The book said there was nothing wrong with things that please both partners. There was even a part about a person who liked the smell of leather. That book went so far as to discuss the use of leather wrist and ankle restraints.

After reading the book, Sandy was almost convinced that she wasn't perverted. She gave it to Paul and, after he read it, they talked. Paul sensed that there was something that Sandy was trying to tell him and he was very curious.

"Are there any things about sex that you would like me to know?" he asked.

Sandy blushed but couldn't answer.

"Something that's mentioned in the book?"

Paul was amazed that someone who was usually so open about sex was so embarrassed. She was obviously hiding some fantasy that he felt sure could provide some extraordinary pleasures. He only needed to find out what it was.

"Why don't you just slip a bookmark in the section and I'll take it from there."

Sandy debated all the next day. Could she take the risk? Would Paul think that she was too far-out? Would he laugh at her?

She took the risk. She dog-eared the page about the person who was into leather and put the book on Paul's bed.

The following evening, while they were lying in bed after making love, Paul whispered, "Leather?" He felt Sandy shiver. "Okay. You don't have to say anything more. Leave everything to me."

Sandy couldn't decide whether to be thrilled or afraid. Obviously, Paul hadn't rejected her. But what now? Despite her jangling nerves, she soon fell asleep.

Paul thought about little else the next day. He was thrilled Sandy had trusted him so much that she had told him a secret that obviously affected her deeply. Leather didn't seem so kinky to him. If the smell and feel of it could turn Sandy on, great.

Paul left work early and went shopping. He remembered seeing ads for leather bondage equipment in a catalog he had received in the mail, and he intended to order it, but for now he would settle for what he could buy at the local mall. He selected a couple of soft leather belts, a pair of buttery-soft leather gloves, and a biker-style jacket he had had his eye on for months, long before he found out about his wife's fantasy.

That evening, after dinner and wine, Paul and Sandy

went into the bedroom and watched TV for a while. Mid-evening, Paul knew it was time to begin to fulfill Sandy's fantasy. He was sure that he had understood what she wanted. If not, he assumed that she would help direct him.

"I bought something today," Paul said, "that I think you'll like." He pulled a box out of a shopping bag and opened it. He withdrew a dark brown leather jacket. "What do you think?"

As the box lay open, the whole room filled with the smell of fresh leather. Sandy closed her eyes and took a deep breath. When she opened her eyes and saw Paul in the jacket, she was in heaven. He looked sensational.

Slowly, he bent down and pulled the gloves from the bag. He slipped his hand into one glove and very slowly pulled the leather down over each finger. As he did so, Sandy's eyes never left his hands. She watched, mesmerized, as he followed with the second glove.

"Now," Paul said. "I think you should be undressed."

Without a word, Sandy quickly stripped out of her clothes. She stood beside the bed, unsure of what to do next.

"Come here," Paul said. There was a forcefulness in his voice that hadn't been there before.

Sandy walked around the bed and into Paul's arms. He held her naked body against the jacket and rubbed his gloved hands over her back and down over her buttocks.

Sandy's nipples rubbed back and forth across the leather jacket as the smell enveloped her. With Paul's hands on her back, it was as if the leather surrounded her. She was more aroused than she ever remembered being, and they hadn't even kissed.

Paul reached up and grasped Sandy's shoulders. He held her away from him and said, "Just two more things, then we're ready."

He pulled out the two wide, soft belts. One he quickly fastened tightly around Sandy's waist, the other around her head, across her eyes and nose like a blindfold. "Now," he said, "you can't see, so you can concentrate on the smell and the feel."

He lifted his wife up and placed her on the bed. She was in another world, one where there were only the sound and feel of Paul and the smell of the leather. She was afraid she would climax just from that.

A few moments later, she felt the bed move as Paul lay down beside her. As he pressed his hands and body against her, she could feel that he was naked except for the jacket and gloves.

"Does this feel good?" he purred. "Can you smell the leather that covers you?" He rubbed one gloved hand over her belly, the other up and down her spine, tugging at the belt around her waist with every stroke. "Can you feel how tight this belt is, this leather belt that tightly grips your waist?" He pulled the belt one notch tighter.

"Oh yes," Sandy whispered. "So good, so tight."

Paul's mouth was so close to Sandy's ear that she could feel his breath as he spoke. "It feels good when I rub your body with my gloves. Now I am going to squeeze your tits, like this," he said as he pinched her already-hard nipple. He kneaded her breasts, alternating his pinches from one to the other.

"Now open your mouth so that you can taste the leather as I rub my fingers over your lips."

Sandy opened her mouth as Paul traced the outline of her lips with his leather-covered finger. She reached out with the tip of her tongue and tasted the glove. Between the feel and the smell and the taste, Sandy was in ecstasy.

"I'm going to make you come now," Paul whispered in her ear. "It's going to be so easy because you're so excited." He pulled off one glove and dipped his naked finger into her soaked cunt. "Yes, so easy."

Paul rubbed her cunt lips, then concentrated his stroking on her clit. "Your eyes are still covered," he murmured, "so concentrate on the smell of the leather as you come." He rubbed her the way he knew would make her climax, and it did.

Sandy came—not the sweet rushing sensation she was used to but a pounding, urgent orgasm that seemed to go on forever.

"Oh yes, baby," Paul said. "Come for me."

"Fuck me now!" Sandy yelled. "Fuck me good!"

Paul rolled on top of Sandy and rammed his cock into her. It took only seconds until he, too, climaxed.

"Oh God." He panted. "That was amazing."

"Amazing," Sandy said. "You are wonderful. You understood so well."

"Ummm," Paul said. "Just wait. I have so many more ideas. I placed an order from a catalog today. A package will arrive in the mail in a few weeks. You may open only one corner of the package so you can smell the contents, but you may not look inside. I can assure you that we'll both enjoy what's inside."

Smell triggers memories as no other sense does. Have you ever gone back to someplace you previously visited and had an attack of nostalgia even before you arrived? It may well be the smell of saltwater or factory smoke or even air pollution. I grew up in New York City and even now when I visit the city in the summer, the smell of hot streets and uncirculated air immediately brings back memories of my childhood.

In the first chapter of this book, Carol uses the smell of a scented candle to bring back wonderful memories. In a later chapter entitled "Then Do It," Ginny uses a pine pillow, among other things, to recapture past loving. For Marcy and Alan, the smell of the seashore releases sweet memories.

MARCY AND ALAN'S STORY

On their honeymoon, thirty years earlier, Marcy and Alan had stayed in a small hotel on the Connecticut shore. As a special gift for their parents' anniversary, the couple's three children had snooped, prodded, and pried and had, as faithfully as possible, planned the same trip. Now, Marcy and Alan followed their children's instructions and drove along Route 1 toward the hotel where they had a room reserved for the weekend.

"Connie said that it's not really the same hotel," Marcy said. "I found I was really sad when she told me that the Middle Beach Hotel burned down about ten years ago. I hope this one isn't a sterile high rise."

"We'll find out soon enough," Alan said. "Here's the turnoff. The kids are pretty resourceful and they put a lot of planning into this thing. We'll have to trust their judgment."

As they drove, the smell was the first indication they were nearing saltwater. "Just inhale that," Marcy said, taking a deep breath. "I had forgotten how wonderful the salt air smells."

"I used to spend my summers on Long Island and it smelled just like this. I feel younger just inhaling."

"Hold that thought, darling," Marcy said. "You were a sexual lunatic when you were younger, and I'd love to meet that man again."

"You know what?" Alan said. "Me, too."

They talked for a moment and lamented that their sex had become perfunctory over the years. "There's no reason we can't start now to recreate some of the things we used to do," Alan said.

"No reason at all."

As they turned a corner, they saw the hotel. "Wow. The kids did well. It looks so much like the one we stayed at thirty years ago," Marcy said. "Little individual buildings, all connected, with a main house where the meals are served. Fantastic."

They registered and were shown to their bungalow.

"It's sensational," Alan said. They hugged and changed for dinner.

After dinner, similar in many ways to the food they had had thirty years before, they found a congenial couple who were looking for a bridge game and they all played for most of the evening. When they got back to their room, they opened the windows, snuggled under their covers, and slept.

Alan was awakened by the warmth of the sun across his face. Without opening his eyes, he took a deep breath. God, that smell is wonderful, he thought. And the sound of the waves and the seabirds. It's just like when I was a kid, just like our honeymoon. Suddenly, he remembered how he had awakened Marcy that first morning after they were married.

Carefully, without waking her, he maneuvered around under the covers until his head was level with Marcy's pussy. Then he blew a stream of warm air onto her mound. Without waking, she shifted her position. Alan kept blowing and repositioning himself as she moved until he was between her spread thighs. He was already very excited, his cock hard and hungry.

He opened his mouth and breathed more warm air onto her beautiful cunt, then pointed his tongue and softly licked. He tasted her characteristic salty taste. She was so wet. Then he knew. "You're awake, aren't you?"

"I won't tell if you won't. Don't stop, whatever you do. You feel sensational."

He grabbed her hips and lapped at her fragrant flesh, feeling her get more and more excited. He recalled that on their honeymoon he had just slid his body up and inside of her. Did he want things to go that fast, with so little actual foreplay? He knew he did and he hoped Marcy did, too.

He licked for another moment, then moved up until his body was covering hers. He heard her purr and felt her hands kneading his buttocks, pulling him to her. He slipped his hard cock into his wife's hot body and thrust several times.

"Yes, darling," she cried. "You feel so good. Make it feel good."

He wanted to wait, tease Marcy and give her pleasure, but he was too excited. He came quickly.

"I'm sorry," he said as he lay on top of Marcy. "It was so fast. Everything about this morning seemed to conspire to make me so horny. The waves and the birds. The feeling of the sun through the open windows. The smell of the salt air and the smell of your luscious body."

"I know. I feel like a teenager again, too. It's fantastic."

"But it was too fast for you. You didn't come."

"I got so much pleasure out of the feeling of your pleasure that my orgasm was unnecessary." She paused. "But, if you're really penitent, you can make it up to me tonight."

Alan grinned. "You mean I have to wait until tonight? What about lunchtime?"

I remember many years ago, during the television coverage of the Olympics, two athletes demonstrated the sports in which the ancient Greeks competed. For the performance, they were dressed in the Greek fashion, wearing nothing but loincloths. The sight of well-developed bodies, oiled and sweaty from physical exertion, was an incredible turn-on for me. Something similar happened to Paula in our next story and it was especially exciting for her since it was so unusual, both in terms of sight and smell.

ARTHUR AND PAULA'S STORY

Arthur and Paula had been married for fourteen years and their sex life, while not terribly varied, was satisfying. Once or twice a week before going to sleep, Paula would snuggle against Arthur's body and wiggle her hips in "just that way" or Arthur would kiss Paula's neck in the sensitive spot where her neck met her shoulder. Arthur and Paula would caress and fondle each other and when they could wait no longer, Arthur would plunge into Paula's hot body. Usually, Paula would climax first, but if she didn't, Arthur would stroke her after his orgasm until she came.

Arthur was a computer programmer who worked for a large commercial company and Paula was a financial analyst at the same facility. Since they drove to work together, every morning they jockeyed for position in the bathroom. They both showered and while Arthur shaved and splashed on his favorite after-shave, Paula put on her makeup. Then they dressed in proper business attire, gobbled a quick breakfast, and drove to work.

In the evening, they met after work, drove home, and, except for rare instances, Arthur showered again and shaved off his exceptionally heavy five o'clock shadow while Paula changed into leisure clothes.

Childless, they devoted a great deal of time and energy to their large home just outside the city. One Friday in late spring, Arthur took the day off from work to direct and assist a crew moving shrubbery around the grounds of their well-manicured backyard. Paula drove to work alone and drove home again in the late afternoon. As she arrived at the end of the driveway, she stopped to allow the gardener's truck, loaded with tools and leftover shrubs, to leave. Still in her high heels, Paula walked around to the back of the house to see the changes the day had produced.

"Arthur," she yelled, crossing the yard and scanning the newly arranged greenery, "things look great." At first, she didn't see her husband. "Arthur, where are you?"

"Here," Arthur called from a secluded spot beside the back door. "I'm just finishing with this azalea."

Paula turned and saw Arthur in a pair of old faded jeans and work boots. Sometime during the warm afternoon, he had pulled off his shirt. As he stood up and admired his new shrub, Paula admired Arthur. God, she thought, he's got a beautiful body, a smooth, hairless chest, narrow hips, and great shoulders.

"Did you notice," Arthur said, walking toward her and pointing to some trees, "how these new dogwoods and white pines shelter the part of the yard where you're standing? Now this section can't be seen by any of the neighbors. Good for sunbathing." He grabbed the backs of two lounge chairs from the patio and pulled them onto the grass near where Paula was standing.

As Arthur got closer, Paula could smell the sweat that made his body slick. That tang was mixed with the smell of earth and green growing things. "Yeah. It all looks good," Paula said, her voice soft and breathy, her eyes not leaving Arthur's body.

Arthur leaned over and placed a kiss on his wife's cheek. He was surprised to notice that she purred and closed her eyes. He moved his mouth to her lips and kissed her again, the kiss long and soft. "Let me take a shower," he said. "Then I have a wonderful idea."

Paula inhaled the smell of sweat, so masculine and, for Arthur, so unusual. "Unh-unh. I like you just as you are." She slid her hands over Arthur's chest, making pathways in the sweat and dirt.

"But, baby, I must smell like a locker room." He ran his hand over his cheek. "And I feel like old sandpaper."

Paula's hands had reached the back of her husband's neck and she pulled his face toward hers. "You claim that no one can see us here," she whispered. "Forget the shower and let's test that theory right now." She reached down and unzipped her suit skirt.

As Paula placed her skirt on one of the lawn chairs, Arthur looked down at his grimy body and filthy hands. He couldn't touch his wife with those hands, but since his laborerlike body seemed to excite her, he didn't want to wash too much. He spotted the hose where he and the gardening crew had left it and used it to wash the worst of the dirt from his hands.

Paula, dressed in her blouse and slip, stockings and high heels, walked up behind him and nibbled on his upper back. Arthur turned and looked his wife over. "You're so clean," he said, his breathing heavy.

"So dirty me a little."

"Are you sure?"

Paula nodded. Arthur wrapped his arms around her and slipped his hands to the back of her neck. As his hands, still cold and damp from the hose water, touched her hot flesh, Paula gasped and pressed her silky blouse against his sweaty chest.

"Yes," she purred, "oh *yes.*" She pressed her mouth against his and again smelled his musky, sweaty scent. It was so unlike her squeaky-clean husband and so sexy.

Arthur began to unbutton the back of his wife's blouse as his lips slid across her cheek and down her neck. Paula could feel the rough texture of Arthur's lightly bearded cheek. Where it touched, her skin tingled. "God, you feel so good."

Quickly, without taking his lips from Paula's neck and shoulders, Arthur unbuttoned her blouse and pulled it off. Her slip, bra, and panties followed. Never had he appreciated her irritation with panty hose so much. He stepped back and looked at his wife, her eyes glazed and her breathing labored.

On a whim, he leaned over and brushed his whiskered cheek over her breast and nipple. She sucked in a breath and arched her back to press her globe more tightly against his face. Arthur could feel her erect nipple against his cheek.

He turned slightly and pulled the tight bud into his mouth, alternately sucking and teasing the tip with his teeth. After a few moments, he stood up and reached for his belt.

"Let me," Paula said. Her hands shaking, she undid his belt, unbuttoned his jeans, and pulled them down, along with his shorts. She tried unsuccessfully to unlace the boots, then tried to get the legs of the jeans over them. Quickly, she ran out of patience. "Sit there," she said, pointing to a lawn chair.

Arthur stretched out in the chair and waited for her to resume work on untying his boots. Instead, Paula straddled his body, her breasts sliding over his slick, smooth chest; her hot pussy was just inches from his huge erection. "You feel so good, I just can't wait." She lifted her body slightly and settled herself on his penis.

It was a strange and erotic feeling for Arthur. His wife was fucking him and he loved it. His ankles were still trapped in his work boots, jeans, and shorts, but he lifted his hips as much as he could, trying to bury his cock more deeply in his wife's body.

They were both so aroused that their lovemaking was brief. With Arthur's hands pulling on Paula's nipples and her hands rubbing over his chest, their hips pounded together and they came almost simultaneously.

Minutes later, still lying together on the lawn chair, Paula started to regain her composure. "I don't know what came over me," she said, now slightly embarrassed by her aggressive behavior. "It must have been that smell of sweat and musky maleness. You were just so sexy, I wanted you so much."

"Don't apologize, darling," Arthur said, snuggling her closer. "I just wonder what I'm going to do with all my cologne and after-shave lotion. Knowing what the smell of sweat does to you, I'm surely never using any of that stuff again."

5

IF IT TASTES DELICIOUS...

I can hear what you're saying. "Now she's going to get silly. She's going to talk about whipped cream and hot fudge."

Well, you're right on both counts. First, I am going to get silly. What's wrong with that? Silly means having fun, laughing, and relaxing, and that's what sex is all about. It also means a bit of embarrassment, which I have found heightens awareness and can lead to marvelous new experiences.

And you're right on the second count, too. I am going to talk about whipped cream and hot fudge. It's too bad that they have been jokes for so long, because that stifles some remarkable creative thoughts. On a recent episode of "Golden Girls," Dorothy accused Blanche of doing kinky things with ice cream toppings. Everyone in the audience laughed, but Blanche wasn't sure that there was anything wrong with that type of fun in the bedroom. I'm with Blanche.

There are several reasons to play with flavors. Some people don't like the taste of sex. Body secretions have a distinctive salty tang that appeals to some and not others. If you find that taste offensive, oral sex, which is delicious to many, may be difficult, if not impossible, for you. Sometimes a person is reluctant to try oral sex, wondering whether she'll like it or be so turned off that she'll interrupt an ongoing love-making session. An introduced flavor is a way to try oral sex with lower risk of being offended.

Another reason to spread hot fudge or some other treat around is to encourage licking. The tongue is a sex organ, both for the user and the receiver. The feel of your partner's tongue on your body is quite different from the feel of hands and fingers. And stroking your partner with your tongue is a marvelous experience.

Spread some honey or jelly on your partner's body— anywhere, not only the genitals. Then lick it off very slowly. Appreciate the taste of the substance as it mixes with the taste of your partner. Then trade places. Lie back and luxuriate in the feel of your partner's tongue giving you pleasure. Pour bubbly wine in a concave part of your partner's body and enjoy the way it tickles your tongue and your partner's skin. Make it very cold.

There are a few things about wine, hot fudge, and such that might be distracting. First, be careful about the bedding. Spread a large towel over the bed to absorb any spills. It's distracting to make love in a puddle. If you are planning to get very messy, a plastic sheet under the towel can prevent you from having to change the linen before you go to sleep.

Watch what you spread on mucous membranes. Some substances can be irritating and will stimulate an allergic reaction. Take care with things very spicy, acidic, or alkaline. Anything that irritates your partner's lips when eaten will probably irritate other membranes. Adverse reactions can occur at inopportune moments. Many years ago, I discovered that my vaginal membranes react badly to the green coloring material used in some bubble baths. Anything's possible. Therefore, be prudent. Test a bit of a substance first to see whether any adverse reaction occurs. I know this sounds a bit clinical but it's necessary. And, of course, take care with any substance that has an abrasive texture and anything very hot or very cold, for obvious reasons.

There are many commercially available products that may appeal to your sense of taste. There are edible love oils and gels, some of which even get warm when you blow on them. And they come in every flavor from strawberry to cinnamon, most tasting like fruit Jell-O. For those of you who want to experiment with edibles, there are Kandie Kondoms (for eating, not protecting) and even an edible cherry-flavored bikini. If you can get a hold of an adult catalog or get to an adults-only store, sample several different products. It will feel silly, but as Glen found out, it can be worth the effort.

GLEN'S STORY

Glen and Barbara had lived together for three years. They thought they would get married eventually, but for now their monogamous arrangement suited them both.

Their sex life was varied and satisfying, except for one thing. Glen had always wanted Barbara to take his penis in her mouth. On a few occasions, he had mentioned it to her and she had done her best to please him. But he always felt that she was putting him in her mouth only to make him happy and that she wanted it to end quickly. He didn't pursue it.

One evening, he was reading a catalog of sex toys and he found an ad that intrigued him. "Lip-smacking Love-Gel," it read. "Hypoallergenic, nonstaining lubricant for lovers. Specify strawberry, orange, or chocolate flavor."

Barbara is a chocoholic, Glen thought. Maybe this is a way to make my fantasy real. Without discussing it with her, he sent for a jar of chocolate-flavored lubricant, using his office address. When it arrived, he stuffed the unopened package in his briefcase and hurried home. Later, in the bathroom, he opened the plain brown wrapping and unscrewed the top of the jar. The smell of chocolate assailed him. He dipped a fingertip into the jar and tasted: chocolate.

Later that evening, he and Barbara were in bed, naked. He kissed her deeply, letting his tongue roam the surfaces of her mouth. Without releasing her lips, he swirled his fingers around her breast, letting his fingers graze her nipple. As it hardened, he sucked it, then rolled over. "I got something in the mail today," he said. "I ordered it for a gag." He handed the jar to Barbara.

"You're kidding," she said with a grin. She opened the jar and inhaled. "Wow, it does smell great."

"Let me try some," Glen said. He dipped his finger in the gel and licked his finger. "It does taste chocolaty." He dipped his finger into the jar again and rubbed some of the gel on Barbara's nipple. Then he bent his head and sucked. "Not bad," he whispered.

Barbara was lost in the sensations. She loved it when Glen sucked her breasts. Heat spread through her body, making her wet and hungry.

Glen dipped his fingers in the gel again, parted Barbara's legs, and spread the goo on the folds of her vagina. Slowly, he ran his tongue over her flesh, lapping up the chocolate taste. Twice more, he dipped his finger in the gel, spread it over Barbara's flesh, and licked it up.

Glen's tongue was giving Barbara exquisite pleasure. As her hips began to move against his mouth, he sat up. "Would you like to taste some?" he asked.

Without waiting for an answer, Glen touched his finger to the gel and held it in front of Barbara's lips. When she opened her mouth, he gently inserted his finger.

"Ummm," she purred. She swirled her tongue over the tip of his finger and he slowly pulled it back, then pushed it further in.

He was fucking her mouth with his finger. Could he take the final step toward what he wanted? He had to try. "More?" he whispered.

Barbara opened her eyes as Glen dipped a finger full of the gel and spread it on the end of his erection. "Taste it for me," he said.

He moved so his cock was level with her mouth, then watched as her tongue slipped out from between her lips and pressed very lightly through the gel on his cock. "Delicious," he heard her say.

Her tongue swirled over his cock, tasting the chocolate and licking up every bit. As she sucked and licked, he spread more gel higher up his penis until Barbara had almost his entire penis deep in her mouth. He looked down at his girlfriend's head bobbing in his lap. She seemed to be enjoying what she was doing. Maybe she was enjoying the flavor; maybe she was loving the pleasure her mouth was giving him. It didn't matter. The fact was that it was the first time she had seemed to get any pleasure out of sucking him.

For Glen, it was heaven, but it was almost too much. He didn't want to spoil anything by ejaculating into her mouth. He pulled back and positioned himself between her thighs. With one stroke, he was inside of her, feeling her slippery wetness. He reached between them and touched Barbara's clitoris. As she climaxed, he could feel the waves of muscle spasms squeezing his cock. He couldn't hold back any longer and he came.

Later, when they had calmed down, he asked, "Was that okay?"

"It was wonderful," Barbara said. "I know you've always wanted me to do that, but until now I couldn't. I don't know why, it just felt wrong. But that chocolate stuff was delicious." She thought a moment. "I guess it made your cock taste like candy, not like something forbidden."

Glen smiled. "The gel comes in other flavors, you know."

"I guess we'll have to try them all. Sort of a taste test."

"Ummm. Yeah."

Since there's not a lot more to say about taste, I thought I'd sneak in another topic. Since aphrodisiacs are usually taken by mouth, I'd like to discuss that subject here. Let me first tell you a story about how to use the ultimate aphrodisiac, the mind.

FRED AND SALLY'S STORY

Fred had noticed Sally the first day she appeared in his Shakespeare class at the junior college. He would have had to be blind not to. She was five foot nine, with long blond hair and big green eyes. Her skin was ivory and her figure was perfect. She would never be interested in the likes of him, he thought.

Fred was a brilliant student with a straight A average in both English and chemistry, but that was where his campus success ended. He had a few casual friends, all male. Girls were usually nice to him and treated him like some kind of pet, but they would never have considered going out with him.

Sally was no different. She quickly became friends with most of the students in the class, including him.

"Hi, Fred," she would say as she took her seat two rows behind him. "How're things?"

"F-f-fine," he would stammer. She would turn to her neighbors and chat until class began.

After the midterm, everything changed. Fred got his usual A+ and Sally failed abysmally. When she got her paper back, he heard her say, "I've got to do something. My scholarship goes down the tubes if I don't pass this course."

"Hey, Fred," one of the other students called, "did you get your usual?"

Slightly embarrassed, Fred nodded.

"Why don't you give Sally some help after school?" his classmate suggested.

"Don't do that," Sally protested. "I'm sure Fred has better things to do with his time than get me through this class."

Better things to do? Fred thought. There isn't anything better in the whole world than to have Sally to myself. His mind whirled. Sally, all to himself.

"Sure," he said, turning to look at Sally. "I could tutor you a few times."

Sally beamed. "You would? That's great."

They met briefly after class and Sally agreed to go over to Fred's house a few evenings later.

Fred knew what he had to do. He contacted a friend of a friend of a friend who met him on a street corner and sold him a bottle of a special formula liquid from South America. Love Slave, it was called. He read the directions over and over, even tasted a tiny drop to see whether the flavor could be hidden. There was no taste.

Fred thought that the bottle probably contained just colored water, but anything was worth a try. Sally, his love slave. It was worth what he paid for the liquid just to think about her that way. But for what it had cost him, it just might work. And anyway, what did he have to lose?

Sally arrived at Fred's house early the following evening, her arms loaded with books. She looked even lovelier than he could believe in a red sweater over a white man-tailored shirt and tight stone-washed jeans. She wore very little makeup, which allowed Fred to study her flawless skin.

For several hours, they poured over *Julius Caesar* while Fred explained the history of Rome and how many of the speeches reflected the thinking of the time.

"All that Roman politics and all those politicians. But, you know, Fred, you make it easier. I think I'm actually beginning to understand some of this. Can we take a break?" she asked.

"Sure," Fred said, rubbing the back of his neck, "Can I get you a Coke?"

"That would be swell. Thanks. I really don't mean to impose."

Fred went into the kitchen and poured Sally a Coke. He dropped in lots of ice, then added exactly seven drops of the magic liquid. He started to close the bottle, then reconsidered and added one more drop.

Thoroughly bored with Shakespeare, Sally glanced up at the living room mirror and saw the reflection of Fred in the kitchen. She recognized the flaming purple bottle in his hand. *Love Slave.* How could anyone believe in that stuff? She watched as he poured some of the liquid into her drink. That's so silly, she thought. But then she thought about Fred, and what he was planning. He's really very sweet, she thought, and he wants to make love to me.

Sally was not new to sex, and she enjoyed it tremendously. However, in her previous relationships she had never been able to totally relax during sex. She concerned herself with her partner's pleasure, often at the expense of her own. Secretly, she had always been intrigued by the idea of being free to enjoy, to let anything and everything happen without worrying about her partner.

Complimented and very turned on by the idea of becoming Fred's love slave, Sally decided to play along.

Trying not to shake, Fred walked back into the living room and handed Sally the Coke. He watched as she drank most of the glass.

"I was thirsty. Thanks. None for you?"

"Not right now. Tell me about yourself." Good, he thought. Make her do the talking. Then I can tell whether anything's happening. Fred realized that he wasn't sure exactly what would happen, but he would observe her and hope.

Sally talked about her family and how she had saved her money, left home, and moved here to live with some relatives to take advantage of a small scholarship to junior college. "I have just enough with my scholarship and my job. If I don't pass this course,

my folks will kill me and my scholarship will disap-
pear. I'll have to leave school and go to work."

Fred noticed that her face was flushed, the pink of
her cheeks accenting the green of her eyes. He was
about to ask her what led her to take Shakespeare
when she asked, "Is it warm in here?"

"Not really," Fred answered, "but why don't you
take off your sweater?"

Sally stood up and removed her sweater, exposing
the stark white of her shirt. Fred noticed that she was
a bit unsteady on her feet. She sat back down but
seemed unable to get comfortable. She squirmed
and rubbed her thighs together.

"Is anything wrong?" Fred asked, hoping that he
was seeing the magic at work.

"I feel funny, hot all over," she said. "It's like I have
an itch that I can't scratch."

"We don't have to get back to work quite yet. Why
don't we talk for a while. Tell me more about yourself.
A girl as pretty as you are must have a lot of boyfriends."

Sally leaned her head on the back of the sofa and
closed her eyes. "Boyfriends? I guess so."

"What do you and your boyfriends do on dates?
Do you go out a lot? Or do you like to stay home and
watch TV?"

Sally stretched her arms out to her sides and spread
her legs. It was several moments until she answered.
"We stay home mostly. Watch TV and make out. You
know."

"Do you let them touch you?" Fred had no idea
what was making him so brave. He was talking about

things that he never would have under normal circumstances. But this situation was anything but normal.

Sally ran the palms of her hands over her breasts. "Ummm. I like it when they touch me."

Fred leaned over and pulled Sally's hands down away from her body. Then he opened the buttons on her shirt and pulled the sides open. Her nipples were fully erect and strained against the lacy fabric of her bra. He felt her pull gently away from him, trying to free her hands. "It's all right," he murmured. "I understand. Let me help you."

He kissed her lips, her face, her ears. He nibbled his way down her neck and across her collarbone. He dropped his head and took one nipple in his mouth through the fabric of her bra.

"Oh God, that feels so good," she said. "Yes. Suck it good." She was on fire and it seemed that only Fred could quench it.

Fred released her hands and she immediately grabbed the back of his head, resting his face more tightly against her swollen breast.

Fred's hands caressed her flesh as he sucked. Then he tried to pull the fabric aside to feel her bare flesh against his lips. He struggled with the unfamiliar garment.

The bra had the clasp in the front and with one twist, Sally unsnapped it and pulled it aside to release her breasts. "Yes, baby," she cried. "Don't stop. I need you."

Fred stroked one and sucked the other, changing positions occasionally. When he dropped one hand to her thigh, he felt her muscles quiver through her jeans.

Sally thought she would jump out of her skin. She wondered momentarily if her excitement really was caused by the aphrodisiac. Then she thought, who cares? I just feel wonderful. "Help me get these things off," she cried, pulling at her jeans. Within seconds, she was naked, spread across Fred's couch. Then her hands were everywhere, pulling at his clothes as he, too, undressed.

He stretched out beside her and stroked her body. She couldn't keep still. She kept running her hands over her own body, then over Fred's chest and back. When she could stand no more, she wound her fingers in his hair, pulled him on top of her, and wrapped her legs around his waist.

He drove inside of her, pounding his pelvis hard against hers. They fucked hard, like animals until, covered with sweat, they both climaxed.

Later, Sally looked at Fred, "I don't know what came over me," she said. "I've never felt like that before."

"I have no idea. I just know it was great."

"That was wonderful, wasn't it?" Sally said. She reached down and held Fred's cock. "And you were terrific. Do you think, with a little persuasion, we could do it again?...I'm still so horny. That stuff you put in my drink really works well."

"You knew about that?" Fred was astonished.

"Of course, silly," Sally said, still stroking Fred's cock. "It only works when both people know about it and it's still working. All I can think about is that I want you to love me again. Right now."

"Are you still my love slave?" Fred asked tentatively.

"I certainly am."

* * *

Wasn't that sensational? Wouldn't it be great if there was a substance that worked that way, that could let you feel free to relax and enjoy sex. I, for one, enjoy losing control like Sally did and abandoning myself to sexual pleasure. And Fred...well he certainly had a great time.

There are no such chemicals that I know of. Hard drugs, such as cocaine and crack, may have some sexual effects, but those drugs are far too dangerous even to consider. Marijuana releases inhibitions, but it fogs the brain, as well. My partner, Ed, a child of the fifties, says that the few times he tried pot, he did get excited, but he couldn't hold a sexy thought long enough to do anything about it. And I, for one, don't want my brain fogged when I make love. I want to remember every detail.

Spanish fly is a urinary and genital irritant. It is actually a crushed meloid beetle and has been thought for years to be a safe aphrodisiac. On the contrary, cantharidin, the active ingredient, is a poison with potentially drastic and irreversible effects.

Yohimbine, a purported male aphrodisiac, is made from the bark of a South American tree. Some articles I've read state that it helps an otherwise impotent man get and maintain an erection, but it's still under study. There are dangerous cardiac and neurological side effects, however, and yohimbine should be used only under a doctor's guidance.

For many people, alcohol is an aphrodisiac, in that it enhances the sexual experience. As long as you don't have to drive afterward, liquor in moderation may help your sex life. It relaxes your nerves and helps tune out some of the outside distractions: the kids, the job, the relatives.

Then there are the foods purported to increase potency. For as many years as there have been lovers, there have been theories about which foods stimulate sexual desire. Oysters, olives, eel, mandrake root, ginseng, and even animal testicles have all been touted at one time or another to increase desire. When I was a teenager, boys used to try to slip an aspirin into girls' Cokes. In later generations, green M&Ms were supposed to make a girl feel sexy.

As I'm sure most of you already know, the primary power of any aphrodisiac is in the mind. If you believe it will work, just about any substance will make you feel sexy. It could be anything from herb tea to a hot dog. But be sure that you let your partner know that you're giving her something that will excite her. Then let her react as she chooses. You may be pleasantly surprised when she goes along with the game and becomes your love slave.

MARION AND DOUG'S STORY

"I bought some very special massage oil today," Marion said to Doug, her husband of twelve years.

"It's supposed to have all sorts of special properties. What say I give you a massage after lunch."

Doug looked up from his Sunday paper and sighed. "That would be wonderful, darling. Work has me all in knots." Doug, a stockbroker, had even spent all day Saturday at the office. "I seem to be so tense all the time."

Marion smiled to herself. She was well aware of how tense Doug was and it had started to put a crimp in their sex life. Recently, they made love sometimes less than once a week, and those rare times were too brief and not very satisfying. But today, Marion had a wonderful afternoon planned, special for both herself and her husband. She had arranged for both their children to spend the afternoon with friends, so they had their house to themselves. Then yesterday, she had bought some love oil in a novelty store, the kind that gets hot when you blow on it. That, combined with the power of suggestion, would do the trick, she figured.

While Marion did a few chores and turned the heat in the house up to eighty, Doug finished his paper. Then they both went upstairs. Marion got a big beach towel and spread it on the bed while Doug tuned the radio to an easy-listening station. "You have no idea what a great idea this is," Doug said as he stripped and stretched out on the bed.

"You have no idea *how* good an idea it is," Marion said. She had taken a few courses in massage at the local adult-education center and she had gotten pretty good. She started at Doug's feet.

Slowly, over a period of fifteen minutes, she worked

her way up both his arms and legs to his back. She spent another ten minutes working on the muscles deep in Doug's back. Then while her hands worked up to his neck, Marion blew on the oil to make it hot.

"What is that stuff?" Doug asked. "It's making my neck hot."

"It is?" Marion said innocently. "I can't imagine why."

"It's gone now," Doug said.

"Turn over."

Doug turned over, still puzzled by the heat at the back of his neck. Marion worked on the front of each of Doug's thighs, then on his chest and shoulders. She glanced at her husband's face and saw that his eyes were closed and he was completely relaxed. As she rubbed the oil on his throat, she again blew on the oil.

"There's that heat again," Doug said.

"I'll confess now, dear," Marion said. "This is special oil. It's really a special love potion that's absorbed through the skin. The heat around your neck is the signal that it's working."

Almost immediately, Marion saw Doug's flaccid penis come alive. She continued. "Now you belong to me. You'll do anything, be anything, just to make me happy." She paused. "Won't you." It wasn't a question.

Doug wasn't sure whether the excitement he was feeling was because of some potion or because of Marion's attitude, but he didn't care. He felt wonderful. Whatever was happening, he'd go along. "I'll do whatever you want."

Marion leaned over and kissed her husband, letting

her tongue roam in his mouth. As they kissed, she thought, This kiss is lasting longer than most of our lovemaking recently. God, I want the old sex back, and I'm going to get it.

Doug reached up and ran his fingers through Marion's hair. He remembered that she always used to love it when he played with her long brown waves. When the kiss ended, he asked, "Maybe you'd like me to brush your hair?"

"Yes," Marion said. "That's a very good idea." She got up and pulled off her clothes. Then she put her shirt back on over her bare skin. "I don't want you to become too impatient."

"Oh, no. Certainly not. I'll do whatever makes you happy."

Marion got her hairbrush, handed it to Doug, and sat on the edge of the bed. Slowly, Doug released the barrette and pins that held her hair off her face. Then he ran his fingers through the strands, massaging her scalp. When he felt her body relax, he began to run the brush slowly through the long tresses.

"God, that feels good," Marion said. "Don't stop."

Doug brushed her hair for fifteen minutes until she finally said, "That's enough for now. I've begun to think about other things. Put the brush away and come around here."

Doug did and Marion pulled him down next to her. "I want you to kiss me," she said. They kissed, their mouths hungry for each other. Then, as he held her face in his hands, Doug kissed and licked her nose and her eyelids. "I only want to give you pleasure," he whispered.

Marion unfastened the buttons that held her shirt and said, "Then kiss my tits. Kiss them good."

Doug did, paying attention to each in turn until her nipples were erect and hard. "Would you like me to service your other needs with my mouth?" he asked.

"Yes. Do that."

Doug knelt between Marion's legs and licked and nipped at the tender insides of her thighs until she was writhing under him. He flicked the tip of his tongue over her clit, then pushed it into her hot pussy. He alternated between soft licks, flicks, and thrusts of his tongue until he thought Marion was almost ready to climax.

"I think you're ready to come, darling. How do you want your orgasm to happen? Do you want my mouth, or my cock, or my fingers?"

"Your mouth and your fingers," she cried.

Doug pushed three fingers in and out of Marion's pussy while he licked at her hot flesh. It took only a few minutes until he felt her juices flow as she came.

When her body finally relaxed, she looked at Doug's erection and said, "You still haven't come, have you?"

"That wasn't your pleasure. There's time for me."

"Yes, right now. Give me your hand." Marion poured some of the oil into his palm. "Now stroke your cock so I can watch you come."

Doug was flabbergasted. Never had he done anything like this with her. But if that was what she wanted, he was only too happy to oblige. He spread the oil over his hard penis and stroked, pulling and milking his cock until he felt his orgasm boiling from inside of him.

"Yes," Marion said, her eyes never leaving Doug's hand, "I want to see your come spurt out. Do it. Make it feel so good that you can't stop. Come for me." And Marion watched as thick fluid spurted from Doug's cock. "Yes, baby," she purred as he spasmed, "that's so good."

As they lay together later, Doug said, "I love that magic love oil. I don't want to know what it is, or why or how. The only thing I need to know is that the oil makes love slaves out of people. Next time, I'm going to rub some on you."

"Yes," Marion purred, "love slaves."

6

IF IT FEELS GOOD...

Touch, the final of our five senses, is in some ways the most obvious. You can't make love without touching, touching with fingers and mouth. When we dream about sex, we blissfully contemplate caressing breasts, erections, and faces. And touch works both ways. Most of us are aware that while you are touching your partner's shoulder with your fingertips, she is touching your fingertips with her shoulder.

To enhance the sense of touch, try making love in the dark. Many people make love with some light on and use the sense of sight as a guide. Turn out the lights. Use your other senses, particularly your sense of touch to "feel" your way along. Be serious or be silly. Chase each other around the bed under the covers—in the dark. Pinch, caress, or scratch whatever you lay your hands on, or your feet or your mouth. Touch with fingertips, palms, the backs of your hands. Touch, touch, touch. Touch each other, touch yourself.

Although touching is an intimate part of making love, many people are afraid to touch themselves during sex, even though it feels wonderful. Although I sometimes masturbated when I was alone, I was reluctant to touch myself during lovemaking until my partner convinced me that he enjoyed watching me. "Show me how you touch yourself," he whispered to me one evening. "Let me watch you give yourself pleasure." I later watched him and derived as much pleasure from watching him as he had from watching me.

I have since discovered that Ed and I aren't unusual. Many men and women enjoy watching their partner masturbate. And masturbation has other benefits. Alex had always wanted to watch his wife masturbate. He knew that if she did, it would relieve him of some of the pressure of pleasing her.

ALEX AND HELEN'S STORY

"Every woman masturbates." Expressed so firmly and at the top of her voice, Laura's statement silenced everyone in the room.

I don't believe the things that come out of that woman's mouth, Helen thought. Laura, who had recently dyed her hair an amazing shade of brassy orange and always wore earrings that looked like small chandeliers, not only could say the word *masturbate* in public but actually believed that everyone masturbates.

"Don't get all quiet on me," Laura said in response to the absolute silence that had descended on the room. "You all know I'm right. I read an article in the beauty parlor today and I believe it. It's not just a male thing anymore. Every woman masturbates."

Helen sank a bit lower in her chair and tried not to be noticed. She felt a flush creep up her back and through the roots of her hair. She glanced around at the other wives as six couples sat and enjoyed coffee and cake after an evening of poker.

"Well," a high female voice piped up, "I don't."

"Bullshit! You do, too," Laura said. "You just won't admit it. And you have real orgasms, not like those fake ones you have at night so Jake will get on with it."

"Laura," the high voice continued, "I think you say and do these things just to see how outrageous you can be."

"I'm not being outrageous," Laura continued. "I'm just stating a fact. Men are allowed to adjourn to the men's locker room and discuss at length exactly how many times they jerked off in the last twenty-four hours and whose boobs they were fantasizing about at the time, but women can't even think about it without being mortified."

She dropped her voice and gave a creditable imitation of her husband's British accent. "Well, you should have seen that cute new bird in the mail room. She had the biggest tits I've ever seen. I had such a hard-on all afternoon that I had to escape to the lavatory and relieve myself."

Everyone tittered and Laura's husband looked totally mortified. Laura's voice returned to its previous strident level. "But let a woman even mention the fact that she occasionally gets physically excited and wants to stroke her own pussy, and it's an outrage."

There was a short silence, followed by three different female voices, each trying to change the subject. Helen pushed her cake plate away and glanced at her husband, Alex. She thought she saw a strange look flash across his face.

She gave him the high sign that meant "Let's get out of here" and stood up to go.

"I hate to break up the party," Helen said. She pointedly looked at her watch. "But I promised to have the babysitter home by midnight." Several other couples rose to leave, as well.

In the driveway, Helen got into the passenger seat of their new Honda, slammed the door, and buckled her seat belt. "Laura really does have a knack for making everyone uncomfortable," she said to her husband, shaking her head.

Alex was silent as he started the engine and backed out of the driveway.

All the way home, Alex was strangely quiet. "Is there anything wrong?" Helen asked.

"Nothing," he said. "Really nothing." He spoke with that particular inflection that Helen recognized. It was his "We'll discuss it later when I've had a chance to digest" tone of voice.

They arrived home and while Helen checked the

children, Alex drove the baby-sitter home. At least everything is fine with the kids, Helen thought. They're both dead to the world.

Helen walked into the bedroom, still puzzled. She pulled off her jeans and shirt and slipped on a light robe. Still confused, she sat at her dressing table and spread cream on her face to remove her makeup.

As she spread moisturizer lightly on her skin, Helen heard the front door close. She heard Alex go straight into the bathroom, his thinking place, and slam the door.

Strange, she thought, very strange. Alex is usually bright and cheerful and, after an evening like this, we usually talk about all the people and the goings-on of the evening.

Alex emerged from the bathroom ten minutes later as Helen was just finishing brushing out her hair.

"Okay," Helen said as he walked into the bedroom. "What's wrong?"

Alex hesitated. "Does every woman masturbate? Do you?"

Helen was speechless. She didn't know what she had expected him to say, but this was the furthest thing from her mind. And masturbation? She didn't know whether every woman did or not, but she knew that she did, frequently. But what could she say?

"Your silence speaks for itself," Alex said, not unkindly. "I always wondered."

She drew a deep breath. "Well, I guess I do, sometimes," she said quietly.

Alex rummaged in his pockets and emptied their contents onto his bureau. He studiously kept his back to his wife. "Sometimes, when we make love, I've thought that you were reaching to touch yourself. I always hoped you would."

Now Helen was truly speechless. Her mouth hung open and her mind whirled.

With his back still to her, Alex continued. "I sometimes feel that I'm entirely responsible for your pleasure. I know that you sometimes fake an orgasm to signal me that I can come. After I do come, you act relaxed, but I know that you're still unsatisfied. I really want to please you but I don't know where to start. I feel guilty somehow." He paused and his shoulders slumped. "I'm saying this all wrong."

"No you're not," Helen said. "Tell me more."

Alex turned, walked over, and sat down heavily on the edge of the bed. "I'm always afraid that I won't satisfy you. I know that sometimes my timing is off, or I touch the wrong spot, or I touch too hard or too softly. I love the look on your face when you come." Alex paused. "Sometimes I wish that you would touch yourself. It would take some of that pressure off me."

"I always thought you'd be insulted. You know, like I couldn't trust you to satisfy me." Helen got up from her dressing table and walked over to her husband.

He wrapped his arms around her waist and buried his face in her belly. "I always wanted to watch you touch yourself. The thought of it is so incredibly erotic. Would you do that for me sometime?"

Helen pulled back and sat on the bed next to Alex. She looked into his eyes. He looked so miserable.

She took his face in both hands and kissed him softly on the mouth.

With a groan, Alex wrapped his arms around Helen's shoulders. He kissed her face, ears, and throat. He pressed his hands on her back, forcing her breasts to flatten against his chest.

Helen held Alex and enjoyed the tingling sensations that his lips and tongue caused. Heat passed from her neck to her nipples, then to her groin. She felt her juices begin to flow and her flesh swell and open.

Gently, Alex pressed her down onto the bed. He parted the front of her robe and opened her bra. He nuzzled at her breasts, licking and nipping at her already-swollen flesh.

"You make me so hungry," he said as he licked and kissed his way down her belly. He flicked his tongue into her belly button, causing a shiver to run up and down her spine.

His mouth went lower, pulling gently at her pubic hair. "Your pussy radiates such heat," he said, "and I love the way you taste."

His tongue began a slow exploration of Helen's vagina, probing and licking deep into the folds and creases. It delved into her dark recesses and withdrew, only to probe again.

He held the globes of her ass tightly to keep her hips still so he could continue to taste her, but he could hardly control her movements.

"Now, darling," he said softly, "let me watch you while you touch yourself. Do it for me, darling."

He took her hand and placed it between her legs.

Over and over, he said, "Do it for me." The heat of his breath caused ripples of pleasure through Helen's body.

Slowly, her fingers slid into her wetness. She used her middle finger to stroke her clit in a rhythm that she knew well.

"Yes, that's good," Alex said. "Do it more."

His face was between her legs and she could feel his cheeks brush her thighs. His fingers held her open so her hand could stroke in its own rhythm.

There was something erotic about touching herself while he watched. And he didn't just watch; he urged her on with his words. "Yes, that's right. Stroke your beautiful body. Do it," he kept repeating. "Let me watch you masturbate."

She could feel her orgasm building. There was no way she could stop now, even if she had wanted to.

"Yes," Alex said, his eyes flicking from Helen's hand to her face. "You're getting close, I can tell. I can see it in your hands and in your eyes. I want to watch you come. And I want to feel you climax."

Without disturbing her rhythm, he slid two fingers deep into her. He held his fingers still so he could feel tiny muscle movements deep inside of her that signaled her impending orgasm.

"Yes." She panted as she rubbed. "Feel it. Now! Right now!" She felt the waves of pleasure travel down her channel and clutch at his fingers. "Share it with me," she said.

He kept his fingers still and marveled at the waves of pleasure that flowed through his wife's body. He had never been able to concentrate on her pleasure before. His cock was hard and demanding, but his pleasure was centered in his fingers and in the look on his wife's face.

For long moments, Helen continued to climax, her breathing ragged. The feeling of Alex's fingers inside of her while her own fingers danced over her skin was the most erotic sensation she could remember ever having experienced.

As the waves of pleasure subsided, Alex turned Helen over so she lay on her stomach. He had always wanted to fuck her this way. If she could take a risk, he reasoned, so could he. He held her hips tightly in both hands and slipped his cock into her soaked cunt from the back.

It was as though her pleasure started all over again but built from that previous peak to new heights. She could concentrate on feeling his increasing physical excitement, since she had already climaxed.

She felt the rhythm of his thrusts increase and the new heat building inside of her. She had never been fucked from behind before, but it was wonderful. It was an entirely new sensation. She could feel that Alex was about to come and the tension in her body became almost unbearable.

He came and, to her amazement, it felt as if she did, too. It wasn't the same kind of orgasm that she had experienced moments before but it was an orgasm, nonetheless. It was almost as if she was experiencing Alex's orgasm.

Later, as they lay together, she chuckled. "And to think that I was afraid you would be insulted."

Alex laughed. "Was it as wonderful for you as it was for me?"

"Better," she said.

"Even the way we made love?"

"That was yummy." She giggled sleepily. "I never realized."

"I feel like we just found a new toy. If I wasn't so tired, I would make love with you all over again."

"There's always tomorrow," Helen said, already half asleep. "Maybe then I could watch you. And the next day, we could experiment with new positions. All kinds of things come to mind."

Alex smiled and cuddled close. "My mind is filled with ideas, too."

They fell asleep still intertwined.

If you think that you might get pleasure out of watching your partner, you may have to initiate things. You may have to take control, insist that your partner touch himself, or you may have to take his hand and hold it while he touched himself. Or he might want to hold yours while you give him pleasure with your hand.

Touch with your tongue. As we learned in the chapter on taste, licking sensitive parts feels terrific on both the tongue and the part being licked. Be aware, however, that some parts that should be very sensitive sometimes aren't. A woman's breasts are constantly in contact with her clothing and eventually become desensitized. Nipples need more active touching, since light, feathery touches are often too delicate to be felt. A little nibble from time to time feels superb. In many men, the tip of the penis is not as sensitive as you might think and needs firmer caresses.

On the other hand, there are parts of your body that are so seldom touched that they are supersensitive. Try licking the inside of your partner's ear or the palm of her hand. Try stroking your partner's underarm, the inside of her elbow, or the back of her knee. And don't overlook one of the most sensitive and erotic areas, the inside of the thighs.

Be aware that your partner may be ticklish. Trying to control giggles can stifle good sex. I, for one, hate to be tickled and it can kill a good mood very quickly, although there are people who find being tickled tremendously exciting. If you get tickled accidentally, don't deny the power of laughter for putting both you and your partner in a relaxed mood.

How well do you know your partner's body? Find out. Set an evening aside and make a tactile map of it. Use your fingertips, your palms, your tongue to get to know all the parts of his body. Which parts are supersensitive? The soles of his feet, the backs of the knees, the insides of the arms. Which need firmer touches? His fingers, knees, elbows. Spend time running your fingers through your partner's hair. How sensitive is his scalp? Once you've mapped his body, you'll know which places are most sensual and which are most erotic, which are ticklish and which are only sensitive to scratches or bites.

Which places give you the most pleasure to touch? And don't touch just with your fingers. Use your palms, your knuckles, your nails. Use the skin of your belly to stroke the skin of her ass. Use your erect penis to stroke her breasts.

Touch goes much further than just your skin on your partner's, however. Let's take the elements of the sense of touch apart and examine some of them and how you can use them to vary your lovemaking.

Texture: Try stroking your partner with a silk scarf, a feather, a cotton ball, then alternate those soft touches with rough surfaces like sandpaper, the bristles of a hairbrush, or your five o'clock shadow. Try making love on warm, soft flannel sheets or cold, slithery satin ones. There's a knack to making love on satin sheets, however, since it's hard to get a grip on the slippery surface with your toes.

Make love in the bathtub, covered with slippery soap, or use a loofah or rough sponge to give your partner a rubdown.

Temperature: During lovemaking, try blowing on an area of your partner's body that is already wet with saliva or love juices. Or allow drops of whatever cold liquid you have by the side of your bed to fall on your partner's overheated skin. Then lick the drops off with your tongue. If you want to use heat the same way, take care not to burn your partner. Drops of liquid wax can smart delightfully. They are hot enough to sting very briefly but cool quickly and won't leave a burn. This activity should be clearly agreed to by both partners before you begin and should be tested periodically.

Heat and cold can be used in another way. I found out how heat-sensitive the genital areas are the first time I tried sunbathing naked. In the privacy of my backyard, I stretched out on my back, with my legs slightly spread. The heat on my vagina was so erotic that I ended up masturbating to a very satisfying orgasm. The genital area is seldom exposed to even slight variations of temperature and so is very sensitive. If you want to sunbathe as I did, however, beware of sunburn. Man or woman, your genitals have probably never seen the light of the sun before and become very painful if even slightly burned.

You can use the sensitivity to changes of temperature in your lovemaking in still another way. There are dildos that are hollow, with corks or screw closures. You can fill them with hot or cold liquid, then stimulate vaginal or anal passages. If you and your partner are into it, it's different and delightful.

I get a particular thrill out of initial penetration when my partner's wearing a condom. He uses the prelubricated kind and the slippery, cold feelings, either vaginally or anally, are terrific.

Temperature can affect lovers in another way. Read about Brian, who loves to make love in the heat.

NANCY AND BRIAN'S STORY

Brian loved the heat. He was at his horniest when the temperature passed ninety. Nancy, his wife, teased that he would like nothing better than to set out a blanket and make love at high noon at the bottom of

Death Valley. Brian would laugh, but he also knew it was true.

In turn, he would tease Nancy that she would probably be too interested in doing push-ups to make love. Nancy would just laugh. Although she was very interested in their sex life, it was true that she did enjoy her daily workouts at the fitness club.

All her exercising and work with weights had their benefits. After years of working out there, her racquet club offered her a job as a fitness instructor, so she quickly took a few courses and got her license. Now she helped people with the machines and occasionally assisted in the free-weight room.

She also got a free family membership. Despite his teasing, Brian had to admit that going to the club after work and doing laps in the pool was relaxing. Following his swim, he would sit and soak in the hot tub, enjoying the heated water and bubbles flowing around his body. Usually, if he soaked long enough, Nancy and whatever guy was on shutdown duty would have the place almost closed up. Then she would be ready to leave with him and they would go somewhere for a bite of dinner.

One evening, Brian walked out of the men's locker room, ready to leave with his wife.

"Sorry, Brian," she said. "Tommy got sick and left early. I have to close up by myself. Can you wait for me for a few minutes?"

"Sure. Is there anything I can do to help?"

"If you wouldn't mind, you could check around the men's locker room and be sure that everything's shipshape. No towels around, showers off, that sort of thing. I'll do the same in the ladies' locker room and meet you out here."

Nancy walked around the ladies' locker room. Everything was in order. As she checked the sauna, she paused. What an idea, she thought. We're the last ones here. Why not? She turned the thermostat up to maximum and set the timer for the maximum, one hour.

She met Brian at the front entrance and turned off all but the night emergency lights. But instead of leaving and locking the door, she pulled Brian toward the stairs. "I've got a great idea," she said. "Let's go stretch out in the ladies' sauna. We can strip off all our clothes, bake for a while and whatever." She raised her eyebrows and grinned.

"Great idea," Brian said, "but will it be okay?"

"Sure, why not. The place is all locked and closed up. And," she paused suggestively, "it's very hot in there."

Brian needed no additional encouragement. He took Nancy's hand and they walked up the stairs and into the ladies' locker room. "I've never been in a ladies' locker room before," Brian said. "It feels so illicit. It smells different from the men's."

Nancy inhaled. The locker room smelled not unpleasantly of a dozen mingled shampoos and body lotions. "I never noticed the smell before. It's nice."

Brian spotted the door to the sauna and opened it a crack. "It certainly is hot in there." He leered at her.

"Don't get any ideas about making love in there. Too much physical exertion can be harmful. We'll just bake for a while and see what happens later."

Brian winked and quickly stripped off his clothes. He and Nancy, who was also naked, quickly grabbed towels and entered the sauna. The heat was intense. Brian, knowing the top shelf was hotter, climbed up and spread his towel. Nancy was content with the lower shelf.

On their backs, Brian and Nancy talked about their day while sweat covered their bodies. Nancy ran her hand over her soaked skin, enjoying the slick feeling. She reached up and ran her hand over Brian's slippery side.

"It's wonderful in here," Brian said. "Makes me think wonderfully sexy thoughts." He caught her hand and used his index finger to make circles in her wet palm.

"Remember what I said about too much strenuous exercise," Nancy warned. She sat up and looked at Brian's body. All of his muscles were totally relaxed except for his penis, which was hugely erect. "The heat really does get to you, doesn't it?"

Brian opened his eyes and saw where Nancy was looking. "Yup, sure does. I must have been conceived in a steam bath."

Nancy ran her hand over Brian's stomach and wrapped her fingers around his cock. "Must have been." She squeezed.

"Don't do that," Brian protested. "You're the one who won't let me get into strenuous exercise in here."

"Who said anything about strenuous exercise." Nancy knelt on the lower shelf and flicked her tongue over the tip of Brian's cock. "I'm just talking about low-impact stuff." She wrapped her lips around the head of his cock and sucked, lowering her mouth slowly to engulf the length of him.

"Oh God, Nancy," Brian said. "I can't take too much of that."

"You don't have to. Just let go."

Brian was astounded. He and Nancy had had oral sex a few times, but she always made it clear that he wasn't to come in her mouth. Did he really understand what she was saying? "If you do that, I'll come in your mouth," he warned.

His cock still in her mouth, Nancy looked into his face. He could see the smile that tilted the corners of her eyes. He relaxed and let the sensations wash over him. Her mouth was heaven. She pursed her lips into a tight ring and slid it up and down his shaft. Then she pulled up so that only the tip of his cock was in her mouth. She created a vacuum while she flicked the tip of her tongue over the end of his penis. It was too much. He came, spurting his semen into her mouth. She swallowed some and some trickled down his penis onto his balls.

Brian just lay there, too exhausted to say anything. Nancy left the sauna, then returned with a cool cloth. As she washed him off, the feel of the cool, nubby material on his heated flesh was enough to get him excited again.

When she saw him begin to get aroused again, Nancy said, "Not yet, darling." She took his hand and led him to the sauna door. "Let's take a shower together, then..."

They didn't leave the club for an hour and a half.

* * *

We can't leave sensations without discussing pain. "Oh boy," I can hear you saying, "now she's really done it. She's going to get into things that are too kinky for me. I'm not interested in the Marquis de Sade, nipple clamps, or whips." As you consider flipping to the next section, you shudder and continue to rant. "And no normal person is into that stuff. The only ones into pain are perverts and weirdos."

Well, you're partly right, but don't turn the pages just yet. I am going to talk about pain. I'm not going to get into anything heavy, but pain can be a powerful sensual tool. You're wrong, however, about who is interested. It's not just perverts and weirdos. In fact, I wouldn't be surprised if, along with all that shouting, there's a prickling sensation in your groin and a little voice is saying, "Don't you dare admit to anyone that you're even a little excited by this. It's too dangerous. And anyway, your partner can't possibly be interested." Hogwash. Keep an open mind and keep reading.

There are a few warnings before we talk about pain, however. Be sure to communicate with your partner before you venture into the use of painful stimuli. If you're sure that your partner's not interested, skip it. Please remember that pain is supposed to enhance lovemaking, not detract from it. And it should never be used to *force* your partner to do anything. But be alert for your partner to "protest too much." Try your best to talk honestly or send clear messages in whatever way you can. And remind your partner to "holler uncle" if anything gets unpleasant. That way, he can yell and protest as much as he wants and not run the risk that you will really stop.

Start small. Have you ever had long fingernails scratched down your back at the height of passion? Feels good, doesn't it? It stems from the contrast between the soft erotic sensations you're feeling in one place and the sharp stabs in another. Well, that's pain in one of its simplest forms. Scratch your partner's back or buns one night and gauge his reaction. It may surprise you and provide a clue as to your partner's desires.

If your partner seems amenable, try a slap across his rump as he climaxes. Both the sound and the feel of that smack can be extremely erotic.

If you are comfortable with the idea that you and your partner are interested in pursuing light pain as an enhancement to a sexual experience, revel in it.

I can tell you from personal experience that some pain is wonderful. But beware, some just hurts. Nipple clamps hurt—a lot. For me, it's not exciting pain, it's just pain. Having my hair pulled during sex also hurts, but it's the kind of pain that makes me hungry. Everyone is different. One person's pleasant pain is another's turnoff. Progress gradually. Communicate. Learn where you and your partner are in the pain spectrum. And, most important, don't make pain during sex an endurance contest, unless you want to. Don't let things go on so long that all the fun has gone out of the experience.

It takes a great deal of trust to allow yourself to get into a painful scenario, and trust doesn't just appear. It must be earned. Both partners must be totally committed to the idea that if one partner "hollers uncle," the activity ends—immediately.

SUSAN AND GERRY'S STORY

It was a New York summer morning. It was still comfortable outside but you could tell that it was going to be a scorcher. Gerry was turning the key to open the front door of his co-op apartment when he suddenly remembered. Damn, he thought, I left my magazine on the park bench. He turned back toward the park. That was a good issue, he thought, and those magazines are expensive and hard to get.

As he jogged back toward the park bench where he had been reading the latest issue of *Spanking and Bondage,* he saw that someone was sitting on the bench, reading his magazine. He slowed to a walk and as he got closer, he realized that the person on the bench was Susan Spencer.

Susan was one of his neighbors in the co-op. They had met almost a year earlier in the local coin-op laundry. While dryers tossed their clothes around, they had sat together and made small talk. They had quickly discovered that they both jogged, they liked the same movies and TV shows, and they both had a love of very hot Indian food. After that, they had met a few times while jogging and Gerry had tried to gather enough courage to ask Susan out. Finally, it was Susan who suggested dinner at Asia House and a neighborhood movie. They had dated for a few months and had finally ended up in bed.

The sex had turned out to be mediocre. Gerry had wanted to confide in her, to tell of his pleasure in toys and sex games, but he had never gotten up the nerve. After a few more dates, they had drifted apart.

Gerry stopped at the water fountain and watched Susan out of the corner of his eye as he pretended to take a long drink. She was so totally engrossed in the magazine that she was unaware he was watching her. He was close enough, however, to see that she was reading avidly, and he was amazed to realize that she was obviously excited by what she was reading.

Gerry didn't know how to handle this situation. He was both embarrassed and aroused. Susan seemed to be engrossed in stories about activities that he enjoyed immensely. Should he let her know that it was his magazine? Could he look her in the eye? On the other hand, could he afford to waste this opportunity? Finally, his excitement won out over his reticence. He slowly walked over to Susan as she read, oblivious to his presence.

Susan had finished her three-mile morning jog about fifteen minutes earlier and had been on her way home when she had noticed the magazine on the park bench. Curious, she had sat down and picked it up. As she flipped through it, she had glanced at the photographs—naked women tied in various positions with sashes, ropes, chains; women with wrists bound with leather, held over the knees of handsome men, being spanked. A sentence in the middle of a story leaped out from the page: "There's no use struggling, dear. You will remain tied until your punishment is over. You've been a very bad girl and...." Susan had become so engrossed that she didn't notice the man approach until she heard a soft voice say, "Excuse me. Susan?"

Startled and embarrassed, Susan slammed the magazine shut and rolled it up, hoping that the man would not see what she had been reading. She looked up and was surprised to see the neighbor she had dated a few months ago.

"Gerry. How are you?" Susan pushed the offending magazine as far from her as she could.

"I'm fine. And I didn't mean to startle you," he said aloud. Tell her now, he thought. Take the risk. "This is a bit embarrassing. I accidentally left that magazine on the bench and was coming back to get it when I noticed that you were reading it and seemed to be enjoying it."

Susan reached over and retrieved the magazine. She looked at the slick paper volume in her hand. As she handed the magazine to him, she stammered, "T-t-this? Oh no, I was just curious." She avoided Gerry's eyes and tried to sound calm and sophisticated. She hoped that he would not notice her trembling.

Gerry gazed at her silently for a moment. Then with a twinkle in his eye, he said, "Well, I must confess that if I had been reading that magazine and you had suddenly appeared, I, too, would have quickly rolled it up and pretended not to be interested in it."

They looked at each other for a moment and

suddenly the tension was gone. "Okay." Susan laughed. "I'm a bad girl and you caught me."

"Let's talk about appropriate punishments for bad girls," Gerry replied, sitting down next to Susan.

The New York summer day was getting warmer and warmer.

Later, they were in one of the bedrooms of Gerry's co-op and he was showing her his collection of erotica—not only photographs and literature but equipment. There were ropes, sashes, velvet cords, and leather straps. There were steel handcuffs and cuffs lined with deep soft fur. There were paddles and whips. The "tails" of the cat-o'-nine-tails hanging on the wall were made of a soft material and obviously would not hurt very much, no matter how hard the "whipping." But some of the others looked as if they might hurt a lot if properly applied. A wooden bench had built-in leather restraints.

Gerry opened a drawer and Susan saw that it was filled with dildos of many sizes and shapes. In the corner of the room was a cabinet that looked like the ones in doctors' offices, containing latex gloves and "medical" instruments.

Susan found the display wildly exciting but also frightening. While she had often fantasized about such things, she had never thought that she might actually consider acting out those fantasies. She knew that Gerry was going to invite her to do exactly that, and she was scared. He had seemedentle, warm, and caring while they had been dating, but this new Gerry was someone she wasn't sure she knew at all.

Weren't serial killers and rapists often described as quiet and sweet? But the room had open windows facing the street. There were lots of people outside. All she had to do was scream if things got out of control. But what if...There were also gags in his collection.

As if reading her mind, Gerry said, "I'm probably almost as uncomfortable about this as you are. This room has always been part of my private fantasy. I've never shown it to anyone before. I guess I've never trusted anyone enough. I've been sure that anyone who knew about this room would think of me as a nut or a pervert. But now that you're here, I can tell you that I would love to act out some of my fantasies with you."

Susan's mind raced wildly. She was more excited than she had ever been before in her life. She desperately wanted to trust Gerry, but how could she trust him to the extent needed to play out these fantasies? What kind of danger was she getting herself into?

"If we do play," Gerry said, "we need to have an 'escape' word so that each of us knows if or when the other really wants to stop. Like the word *uncle.* That way, if I'm holding you over my knee and spanking you, you can beg me to stop, but I won't. But if you simply say the word *uncle,* I will immediately stop whatever I'm doing."

"Uncle?"

Gerry nodded. "Whatever I'm doing, you have my word that I will stop."

"Whatever you're doing?"

"Whatever I'm doing."

Susan had an image of Gerry cuffing her wrists, pulling down her jogging shorts and panties, forcing her over his knees, and spanking her naked ass while she cried for him to stop. She felt herself trembling and was suddenly aware that she was wet between her legs. She wanted it so badly.

Suddenly, Susan knew what she could do to allow herself to trust Gerry.

"I have to admit that this is all terribly exciting to me, but I'm not ready for it yet. The kind of trust I need comes slowly. But I would love to make love to you, without the 'special effects.'"

Susan walked over to Gerry and began unbuttoning his shirt. Soon they were both naked. Gently, Susan pushed Gerry down to the floor. "Lie down and let me do all the work."

Gerry lay on his back on the deep soft carpet covering the bedroom floor while Susan touched and stroked every part of his body. Leaning over him, she brushed her nipples over his mouth, then caressed his entire body with her body. She put his hard penis between her breasts and squeezed them together, then slid them up and down. Gerry's breath became ragged as his excitement grew.

He wanted to touch her, to stroke her, to give her as much pleasure as she was giving him, but whenever he reached out to her, she gently pushed his hands away and said, "Just lie still. I don't want you to come until I'm ready. I want you to tell me if you feel that you can't hold back much longer."

Susan continued to stroke Gerry with her hands

and body, then softly stroked and cupped his balls in her hands. She began to lick and suck his penis—first just the tip, then taking the whole shaft deep into her mouth. Gerry's hips began moving involuntarily and soon he said hoarsely, "Susan, I'm going to come. I can't hold back much longer."

Susan stopped everything that she was doing and looked down. "I'm going to lie on my back now and I want you to slide your swollen cock into my cunt. But once it's inside, I don't want you to move."

Susan lay on her back. Gerry was trembling so much that Susan had to guide his penis into her cunt. Gerry tried to be still but was so aroused that he could not keep his hips from moving.

As he fucked her, Susan said, "I told you to lie still, Gerry. I'm not ready for you to come yet."

Gerry slowed his thrusts but felt that he could not stop. "I don't think I can hold back."

Quietly and very, very gently, Susan said, "Uncle, Gerry, uncle."

As he remembered his promise, Gerry realized what she had done. He gritted his teeth and stilled his hungry body.

Susan and Gerry lay together in the heat of a summer dog day while their breathing slowed and their trembling stopped. Their bodies were wet and slippery. After a while, Gerry's erection softened and he was unable to remain inside Susan. His balls ached as he rolled over onto his back.

Susan propped her head on her palm and searched Gerry's face for anger or resentment, but she found none. Gerry had done exactly as he had promised. Now she knew that she could trust him completely.

"Maybe next time..." Gerry started to say.

"No," Susan said. "What I just did to you was very, very bad. I've been a naughty girl and need to be severely punished."

Gerry saw her mischievous smile and suddenly understood. "You certainly do," he replied, reaching for the fur-lined leather cuffs.

When you're ready to try a lightly painful fantasy as a prelude to lovemaking, you might want to act out a story similar to the one about the teacher and the unruly student that Claire and Arny invented.

CLAIRE AND ARNY'S STORY

Over the seven years of their marriage, Claire and Arny had developed and refined a game they call Dragonsex. It had begun with notes that they had sent to each other while Arny was away on army maneuvers. These notes contained fantasies that they promised they would act out when he returned.

When he got back, they took an old tin that used to contain tea leaves and put the notes inside. Then they drew one out and acted out the fantasy written there. Once a month or so, they drew another one out and played. If they enjoyed the fantasy, they put the note back in the can. Occasionally, when one or the other of them had an idea for a new fantasy, another slip of paper was added to the collection.

One afternoon about two years later, Claire found a pewter dragon with large outspread wings and glued it to the can lid, a symbol of their fantasy life together. Now, with two children, they played Dragonsex only a few times a year.

One evening, Arny arrived home from work, to find Claire on the phone to her mother. "That's so nice of you, Mom," she was saying. "The kids will so enjoy the circus. What time will they be home?"

After a moment's silence, Claire said, "You're sure it's no bother? Arny and I could pick them up."

Another pause. "Okay, then. I'll pick them up around noon tomorrow. And thanks again." She hung up. "Mom and Dad got circus tickets for the boys for tonight. They'll be by in about a half an hour to pick them up. They're going to keep them for a sleep-over."

"You mean we'll have some privacy?" As Claire nodded, Arny's eyes strayed to the pewter dragon can on the back of the refrigerator. "Let's pick now, then we can enjoy the anticipation."

Quickly, Claire grabbed the can and pulled off the lid. Arny pulled out a well-worn slip of paper. Without even reading it, he knew what it said. "Teacher and student." They both smiled. "Let's get the kids ready, then plan."

Three-quarters of an hour later, Claire and Arny sat at the kitchen table. Claire straightened up and a stern look wrinkled her brows. "You know, young man, your table manners have been abominable recently. We really must work on them."

Not knowing exactly what Claire had in mind, Arny said, "What did you have in mind?"

"I think it's time to practice. I think we should go out to a restaurant and have dinner. There, you can demonstrate your good manners while we have a nice meal. If your behavior is perfect, all's well and good. If you make mistakes, however, I'll have to take measures to correct you."

"That sounds great," Arny said.

"Your speech needs work, too. You will address me as Miss Stevens and you will speak correctly at all times."

"Yes, Miss Stevens."

They went to a small, very fancy Italian restaurant they both liked and Claire ordered for both of them. "I hope you remember which fork is which," she said, looking at the salad and dinner fork on the pink tablecloth, "and which spoon."

When the salad arrived, Arny deliberately chose the wrong fork. "You're a surprisingly poor student," Claire said. "How difficult is it to remember the difference between two forks?"

"I'm sorry I've displeased you."

Claire had a gleam in her eye as she said, "Not as sorry as you're going to be."

Later in the meal, Arny purposely stirred his coffee with his soup spoon and earned a glaring look from Claire. "Oops," he said with a giggle. "I fucked up again."

"Mister," she said, her voice low but hard, "your language has just earned you more punishment."

When they arrived home, they walked into the den. "Now, young man," Claire said as she sat in a straight desk chair, "we must talk. I don't want to have to call your parents and tell them what a poor student you are."

"You mustn't do that," Arny said, sounding terrified. "My parents would skin me alive."

"Well," Claire said, "you must be punished. Maybe we can avoid calling them if I punish you."

"Oh yes, anything, Miss Stevens. Just don't call my folks."

"Get me my ruler." She motioned to the desk. Arny opened the top drawer and withdrew an old wooden twelve-inch ruler. Slowly, he crossed the room and handed it to Claire.

"Now, drop your pants."

Self-consciously, Arny opened his belt and let his pants drop to the floor. Claire could clearly see his pulsing erection making a bulge in the front of his shorts. She used the ruler to tap on his underpants. "What's that all about?"

"Nothing, Miss Stevens. Nothing at all."

"It's something, all right," Claire said, "but we'll deal with it later. For now, over my knees."

His pants still around his ankles, Arny hobbled to stand next to his wife and draped himself across her lap, his cloth-covered ass in the air. Claire could feel the bulge of Arny's cock as it pressed into her thigh.

"Now, we must calculate your punishment," Claire said as she rubbed Arny's cheeks. "I noticed two major etiquette errors during the evening and one serious breach of correct language. I think five for each, which makes a total of fifteen. Do you have any problem with that?"

"No, Miss Stevens. I think fifteen is correct." In the beginning, they had spanked each other lightly with an open palm. Soon, they realized that Arny liked to be on the receiving end and Claire didn't particularly enjoy being spanked. Although at first, Claire had spanked Arny because he liked it, now she got pleasure and sexual excitement out of the game as well. Recently, Arny had requested that his punishment be a bit more painful than Claire had been able to do with her hand, so they had begun to use a ruler.

Claire rubbed Arny's cheeks, then suddenly brought the ruler down with a smart whack. Arny jumped. "That's one," Clare said. The next three swats were soft, more noise than feeling, the fifth hard again. The next nine were delivered with varying strength. "One more to go," she said. "This one is for your bare ass. Strip!"

Always before, the swats had been over his shorts or with her bare hand, but now she wanted him to feel this last one. Arny pulled down his shorts and let his erection spring free. Claire again tapped the ruler against his penis. "Spanking seems to agree with you. Now, over my lap."

Arny dropped across her knees, his naked hard cock pressed against Claire's leg. Claire raised her hand and brought the ruler down across Arny's buttocks. Arny stiffened and a red stripe appeared across both cheeks.

"Now you can prove that you've learned proper manners, young man," Claire said. She stood up and removed her panties from underneath her dress. She sat back on the chair with her legs spread. "Come over here on your hands and knees and show my hot pussy that your mouth has learned manners."

Arny crawled over and tentatively flicked the tip of his tongue over his wife's wet cunt. It still amazed him that she became as excited as he did. Skillfully, he licked and sucked and probed and felt Claire become hotter and hotter. "May I use my fingers, Miss Stevens?"

"It's always good manners to ask," she said, panting, "and yes, you may."

Arny used his fingers and his mouth to increase his wife's excitement until, with three fingers inside of her, she climaxed. "Oh God, so good," she screamed as the spasms overwhelmed her. "So good."

As she calmed, Arny licked up her juices, then ran a line of tiny bites along the inside of her thigh. As he felt her body relax, he bit her hard inside of her knee.

"Ow, that hurt," she yelled. "You bit me."

"I certainly did," Arny said, his cock still hard and becoming painful. "And I deserve whatever punishment you feel I deserve."

If you enjoyed that story, slip a bookmark in it right now, before you censor your reactions. Then start slowly, as Claire and Arny did. Take the risk. It's worth it.

7

THEN DO IT...

This chapter contains stories about couples who used all of their senses to bring something new and exciting into their lives. Slip a bookmark into one of the stories for your partner to find or just collect ideas to add to your repertoire. Read and enjoy.

MARTY AND BONNIE'S STORY

Marty and Bonnie had been married for twenty-four years and had three grown children and two grandchildren. Until recently, their life together had been full of sexual adventure and fun.

Bonnie was tall and slender, with a figure that carried clothes well. She was a good-looking woman with salt and pepper hair and large gray eyes. Her breasts drooped and her thighs were slightly heavier than she wanted, but, if she was completely honest with herself, she didn't look half bad.

Marty was of medium height and, despite a slight paunch, he was still the same weight as when he and Bonnie had graduated from college together. He was happy with Bonnie and their life together, but lately he had noticed a change in his wife's behavior in bed. They still made love frequently, but now Bonnie seemed different. She seemed in a hurry somehow, unwilling to wait until she was really excited. She would stroke his erection until he was fully excited, then pull him toward her, saying, "Please make love to me."

Marty finally sensed the truth. His wife was depressed about her impending fiftieth birthday.

Bonnie was well into menopause and, despite all the years of good sex with her husband, she was convinced that once she passed fifty, her sex life would be over. She had read all the articles that maintained sex was not only possible over fifty but could be just as exciting as before, but she knew they were written by people still in their thirties. She watched the antics of the women on "Golden Girls," but she didn't believe that any of that applied to her. Therefore, she spent her lovemaking time making sure that Marty was satisfied, convinced that she could no longer feel the passion that she had when she was younger.

When he confronted her with her misconceptions, Marty was sympathetic but firm. "Your fears are groundless," he argued, to no avail. Although their sex life had been quiet over the previous six months, he appreciated Bonnie's sensual nature and knew what

Bonnie didn't, that the relationship between sex and age was in the mind. So he made plans. He was sure that all he had to do was recreate some of the pleasures they had previously enjoyed and she would realize how silly she was being.

As Bonnie's birthday approached, she became increasingly morose. Marty teased her with hints about a fantastic weekend vacation, but nothing that he could say or do could take the pressure off. Since her birthday fell on a Friday that year, he had planned to drive to Atlantic City and arrive in the late afternoon.

Just before they left the house, Marty handed his wife the first of her presents, wrapped in bright purple paper. Bonnie tore the wrapping off the small box and found three cassettes of songs by Johnny Mathis.

"Remember when we danced to that music?" Marty asked. "It was like making love standing up."

A smile curved Bonnie's lips. She clearly remembered pressing their bodies together in their friend Nancy's living room. "Remember the red scarf that Nancy used to put over the light so we could dance in the darkness?"

"Yeah." Marty sighed. "I also remember when her mother came storming in and made us turn all the other lights back on." He laughed. "As I recall, when we heard the key turn in the front door, Nancy and Fred were draped all over each other on the sofa. They barely managed to get reassembled in time."

Marty and Bonnie, still laughing and reminiscing, got into the car. "Why don't you play one," Marty said, motioning to her new tapes. She unwrapped the

first one and soon the wonderful music filled the
Toyota.

All during the two-hour drive, Bonnie played the
nostalgic music. They arrived, both mellower than
when they had started, and walked into the opulent
hotel lobby. Marty registered and together they went
up to their room, dropped their bags, and went back
downstairs to have dinner.

The food was sensational. Thick steaks, fluffy mashed
potatoes, and a crisp salad were accompanied by a
bottle of rich Bordeaux. By the time they finished
dessert, Bonnie was beginning to enjoy her birthday,
in spite of the terrible number. They adjourned to the
casino. After an hour of playing the slots, they were
ten dollars ahead. Marty suggested they quit while
ahead. As they took the elevator to their room, they
looked at each other with little doubt about what
was on their minds.

Back in their room, Bonnie stretched out on the
bed while Marty rummaged in his suitcase. Withdrawing a small cassette player, Marty unwrapped and put
in the last of the tapes. With the music playing, he
disappeared into the bathroom.

Bonnie heard the water running as she listened to
the wonderful old songs. She hardly looked up as
Marty came out of the bathroom, left the hotel room,
and returned a few moments later with a bucket of
ice.

Minutes later, he called gently, "Come in here,
darling."

Lazily, Bonnie got up, walked over, and opened the
bathroom door. Inside, Marty stood deftly removing

the cork from a bottle of champagne. With a small pop, the cork came free and Marty quickly filled a glass for Bonnie and one for himself. He handed a glass to Bonnie and raised his. "To you on your birthday." He took a swallow. "And to this wonderful evening, which I want you to leave entirely to me."

Bonnie let the cold liquid trickle down her throat. Then she noticed that the bathtub was filled with steaming water. "For me?" She raised an eyebrow.

"Absolutely."

"That's not my usual bath oil I smell," she said, sniffing the steamy air.

"It's another present. I wanted everything to be new and different tonight."

Bonnie inhaled the lavender fragrance of the new bath oil. "It's very lovely," she said. "Not my usual taste."

"Do you like it?"

"Very much."

"Okay. Take off your clothes and climb in."

Bonnie found that between the alcohol she had consumed and the new scent in the air, she felt strangely disconnected from her usual self. She felt almost hesitant about removing her clothes in front of her husband. Her reluctance was compounded by the fact that Marty was fully clothed and showed no signs of undressing.

"Aren't you getting undressed, too?" she asked.

"No. This is your party and I'm here only to serve you. Now let me help you out of your clothes."

Marty stepped behind his wife and reached around to unbutton her blouse. As he did so, he turned her so she faced the huge mirror over the double sink. Slowly, as Bonnie watched, Marty unbuttoned her blouse, revealing her lacy white bra beneath. As he parted the sides of the blouse, his fingertips skimmed her flesh, almost but not quite accidentally.

Bonnie stood transfixed as she watched her husband's hand remove her top. Her arms hung limply at her sides as she pulled the sleeves off over her hands. As the strains of "Chances Are" filtered into the bathroom, Marty turned Bonnie around. He wrapped his arms around her waist and they moved slowly to the music. Bonnie rested her head against Marty's chest, remembering their courtship.

When the music finished, Marty said, "Your bath is getting cold. Let me finish getting you ready." When Bonnie began to get undressed, he said, "Let me do it all."

Piece by piece, he removed her shoes and socks, her slacks, and finally her bra and panties. As she stood naked, Bonnie watched Marty's eyes roam over her body.

Then he broke the spell by turning her around and walking her to the tub. "Climb in," he said.

Bonnie stepped into the tub and sat down, enjoying the feel of the oily scented water. Eyes closed, she sank down and rested her head on the rim of the tub.

Marty set Bonnie's champagne glass on the edge of the tub, rolled up his sleeves, and dipped his hand into the water. Slowly, he poured handfuls of the warm water over Bonnie's shoulders and breasts. He watched her face as he took a new bar of lavender-scented soap and rubbed a facecloth over it until he had a thick lather. Then he began to wash Bonnie's body. He started with her shoulders and arms, sensuously running the soapy cloth over her skin. He spent a long time on her hands, soaping and massaging each finger.

Then he washed each leg, rubbing the cloth up and down her thighs and calves. He soaped his hands and washed her feet, spending time rubbing one finger in and out of the space between her first two toes. It was as if his finger was a cock and he was fucking her foot.

Bonnie remained still, reveling in each sensation. She giggled softly as Marty inadvertently tickled the soles of her feet and she purred as he made love to her toes.

Marty soaped the cloth again and, after dribbling water over her chest, began to rub the lather over Bonnie's breasts. As he washed one, he blew cool air over the other. He knew that the combination of cool and warm was making Bonnie very excited and he watched her nipples swell.

He trickled water over one nipple, then sucked a droplet from the tip. He felt Bonnie shiver with pleasure. He continued to suckle while he slowly rubbed the facecloth over her other breast.

After many minutes, he let the cloth fall into the water and he picked up the wineglass. He raised his head and quickly poured a small amount of the chilled wine over his wife's breast. As the golden liquid flowed down, he licked and sucked so that not a drop fell into the bathwater. He did the same with the other breast, finally rinsing his wife's flesh with the warm water.

The sensations were driving Bonnie crazy. She wanted to move but didn't want to interrupt, so she held her body still and kept her eyes closed.

When her nipples were fully hard and erect, Marty said, "Now lean forward; I want to wash your back."

She did as he asked and smiled as he rubbed lavender-scented soap over her back and down into the crack of her bottom. His slippery finger circled her opening, causing prickles up and down her spine. Neither of them had ever considered anal sex, but her reaction made it seem like a possibility for sometime in the future.

"Now lie back," Marty whispered, taking his hand from her buttocks.

As she lay back, his soapy hands reached down and carefully washed the folds of her vagina, rubbing his fingers over her slippery clitoris. She was in heaven as his fingers explored her body. She could feel the difference between the wetness of the water and that of her juices. She wanted him to drive his fingers into her and was willing to break the spell to pull his hand into her. But just as she started to reach for his hand, he sat back on his haunches and said, "Stand up now."

She stood and Marty, still fully dressed, took a thick towel and, while Bonnie stood in the warm water, rubbed her belly and her back. "I have a better way of drying certain parts of your body," he said. He lifted her foot and placed it on the edge of the tub. His face was level with her vagina. He used his fingers to part her lips and flicked his tongue over her clit, tasting the combination of bathwater and his wife's distinctive tangy taste.

As his tongue drove her wild, Bonnie opened her eyes and saw their reflection in the mirror. There she stood, naked, with her husband orally servicing her vagina. That view was enough to cause her to climax.

"Oh, God, it's so good," she said as the waves of pleasure flowed over her. "Don't stop," she begged as the spasms went on.

When she finally caught her breath and looked at her husband, she saw a huge smile on his face. "Happy birthday, darling," he said. "Now, let's go inside. If you're good, I might take my clothes off and fuck your brains out."

Happier than she had been in months, and totally reassured about her sensuality, she said, "Let's do just that. I'm longing to do wonderful things to you, too."

BILL AND GINNY'S STORY

The idea occured to her at the flea market. Ginny had stopped at a stall with a sign that read THOUSANDS OF TAPES—ALL KINDS—ONLY $1.00. Always eager to add to her collection, she parked Jesse's stroller and began to sift through the baskets filled with tapes by singers and groups she had never heard of. Then she thumbed past a tape called *An Evening in the Piney Woods: White Sound for a Good Night's Sleep.*

Who would be interested in an entire forty-five minute tape of night sounds? She put the tape back into the basket, then retrieved it. Something triggered a wonderful memory. She looked at the cassette box and wondered what had caught her eye. Then she realized that the picture on the case looked very like the cabin that she and Bill had borrowed for their brief honeymoon three years earlier. That was some weekend, she remembered. Nonstop sex from Friday evening until Sunday. They had been so exhausted when they returned to town that they had overslept and had both been late for work Monday morning.

How wonderful it would be if they could recreate that weekend. As she thought, an idea formed in her mind. With a toddler, they couldn't get away to the mountains, but could she bring the mountains to their house?

On a whim, she handed a dollar and the tape to the older man in charge of the stall. He slipped the cassette in a bag and Ginny put the package in her purse. She wouldn't tell Bill about anything just yet.

Ginny and her son continued to wander through the gigantic outdoor market. She would have missed the pine pillow if Jesse hadn't begged to stop so he could "pet the doggy." As he petted a magnificent golden retriever, she glanced at the display in the stall next to her. There it was, a burlap pillow with SOUVENIR OF THE POCONOS—1956 written across it. She picked up the old-fashioned pine pillow, squeezed it, listening to the scrunchy sound. She held it to her nose and inhaled, then grinned. The scent of the needles was exactly what she wanted. Without bargaining, Ginny handed the woman $2.50—the entire amount she asked for—and stuffed the small pillow into her purse with the tape. She pried Jesse away from the doggy and drove home.

During the week, she picked up a bottle of pine air freshener and a pine-scented candle. One afternoon, while Jesse took his nap, she searched through her old summer clothes and found one of the shorts outfits she had worn that weekend. She tried it on and was happy to realize that without too much effort the pants closed. The top, however, was another matter. Since she had only recently stopped nursing, the tank top was a bit tight over her large breasts. Experimentally, she slipped her bra off and enjoyed the way her breasts jiggled under the fabric. She put the outfit away in her drawer and searched for something for Bill to wear. In his dresser, she found a pair of jeans and a T-shirt that he had worn and put them with her outfit.

She planned the "Evening in the Woods" for Saturday night. Jesse shouldn't be any problem, she thought. He had recently started going to bed easily around 6:30 and he usually slept soundly until morning.

Late Saturday afternoon, Ginny sent Bill on an extended errand so she could set up the house. While he was gone, she set up a fire in the fireplace, laid out Bill's clothes, bathed, inserted her diaphragm, changed into her "summer outfit," and fed the baby and put him down. When Bill arrived home, she called to him from the kitchen. "I have a surprise for you. Go into our room and put on the clothes I've laid out for you. Then come into the living room."

"What's up?" he called.

"None of your snoopy snoot," she called back. "Just follow instructions." She heard Bill's laughter as he walked toward the back of the house. When he emerged a few minutes later, he was dressed as she remembered he had been on their honeymoon. IF YOU'RE GOOD AND SAY YOUR PRAYERS, the shirt said, WHEN YOU DIE YOU'LL GO TO TEXAS. She remembered when his brother had sent him that shirt.

"Well," Bill said as he joined Ginny in the living room, "you look fantastic. What's this all about?"

"Do you remember that shirt? You wore it on our honeymoon."

Bill smiled as he recalled that weekend. "I do remember," he said. "That was some weekend. I was exhausted for a week."

Ginny leered. "Well, tonight is 'Honeymoon Revisited Night.' Let me light the fire."

As she lighted the fire, he smelled the wood smoke, and something else. "What's that other smell?"

"Pine. I got a scented candle at the supermarket. Like it?"

"It's great, and so are you." As he pulled Ginny toward him, he noticed her tank top. "You're not wearing a bra, are you?" Without waiting for her to answer, he slid his hand up under her top and cupped her breast.

Playfully, Ginny batted his hand away. "Not yet, buster." She giggled. "Dinner first."

"Okay, what are we having?"

"You'll see," Ginny said as she disappeared into the kitchen. She returned moments later with hamburgers, buns, potato salad, corn, and two bottles of beer. Quickly, she set up the grilling rack over the fire and put the burgers and the corn on to cook. They were drinking their second beer when the meal was ready.

"This is great," Bill said as Ginny spread a cloth on the rug by the fire. "It really is just like that evening in the cabin."

Ginny served and they ate leisurely, half-sitting, half-lying on the floor. Later, while Bill cleaned up, Ginny dished up large portions of Jamoca Almond Fudge ice cream and poured two glasses of Baileys Irish Cream to drink and pour over the ice cream.

Back in the living room, Bill said, "This is heaven. I remember that we barely finished dessert before I ravished your body."

"Last one done is a rotten lover," Ginny singsonged as she devoured her dessert. While Bill put the dessert dishes in the dishwasher, Ginny put the night-sounds tape in the player and put the pine pillow on the floor. As the tape played, she could hear crickets and frogs and the sound of the wind in the pine trees.

Smiling, Bill dropped to the floor next to her and picked up the pillow. "What's this?"

"Squeeze and smell," Ginny said.

"That's fantastic. I've never seen one of these."

"It's called a pine pillow. My grandmother had one and I found this one at that flea market Jesse and I went to last week."

"This is all wonderful. It's also making me very

hungry." Bill pushed his wife backward until she was lying across the tablecloth. He lifted her head and put the pine pillow underneath. Then he leaned over her and pressed his mouth on hers. "Oh, baby," he purred, his mouth still against her lips, "you taste so good." Ginny listened as the sound of her husband's voice mingled with the sounds on the tape.

Ginny slid her hands up Bill's back and through his hair. "You taste so good, too," she murmured. As Bill's mouth moved over her ears and throat, she arched her back and threw her head back.

Bill ran his teeth and tongue over Ginny's collarbone and licked the hollow at the base of her neck. He could feel the pounding of her pulse in her neck and licked the length of the column of her throat.

Ginny wanted to feel skin against skin, so she grabbed the back of her husband's shirt and pulled it up. In moments, they were both naked to the waist, pressing hot flesh against hot flesh. Her hands roamed his body, feeling the play of muscles under his smooth skin. She slid her hands under the waistband of his pants and kneaded his buttocks, pressing his obvious erection tightly against her.

"Oh, baby, you make me so hot," Bill whispered. "I want to fuck you right now and all night." He slipped his hand between them and down the front of her shorts under her panties. "You want that, too. I can feel how wet and hot you are."

"Oh yes, baby, yes." It had been a long time since she had been so excited, so she pulled at her clothes, unable to get them off fast enough. When they were both naked, she wrapped her legs around Bill's waist and impaled herself on his hard cock. As he held his body still over hers, she thrust upward rhythmically, fucking herself with her husband's hardness. "Hold still," she cried, "and let me make love to you like this."

Bill supported himself on his elbows and knees and watched the ecstasy on his wife's face as she devoured his cock. Too soon, he realized that he wouldn't be able to control himself much longer. He also knew what would drive Ginny over the brink, so he bent down and took her nipple in his teeth and bit her, not too gently.

"Yes," she screamed, "right now."

Bill dropped his body onto hers and pounded his flesh into her. Together, sweat-drenched and panting, they came, screaming.

Later, Bill said, "That was incredible. I was horny as a newlywed. The sounds of that tape combined with you screaming was just like that night at the cabin."

Ginny blushed. "I guess I do make some noise. It's lucky that Jesse sleeps so soundly." She paused and listened to the tape that was still playing in the background. "I didn't know you had noticed the tape."

"I was too involved to mention it at the time, but it sounds just like the woods."

Ginny told Bill about how she had stumbled on the tape. "What a great idea," he said. "But the tape lacks one sound that I'll never forget from that evening."

"What's that?"

"The tremendous crash when the raccoons got into

the garbage cans. I remember that we were interrupted just at the critical moment."

Ginny laughed. "I do remember. But that interruption was actually fun. We got to start all over again after we picked up the mess."

Bill rolled onto his side, reached over, and squeezed Ginny's nipple. As he felt the nipple harden, he nibbled at her ear and said, "I guess we did start all over at that."

It was hours later when they finally went upstairs to bed.

AMY AND BEN'S STORY

Amy found the small card next to her coffee cup one Saturday morning. "Your appointment with Dr. Jones is confirmed for 10:00, Saturday the 24th." That's today, she thought, but who's Dr. Jones?

"Ben," she called, knowing he was upstairs in their bedroom, "did you see this card on the kitchen table?"

"Your appointment?"

"Yeah."

"Well," he yelled, "the doctor will see you now."

The wheels started turning. A fantasy about playing doctor was something they had talked about. Ben had recently told her about a fantasy he'd had involving a woman who went to the doctor and sexy things happened. Was he planning to act out that fantasy now? There was only one way to find out. She went upstairs and into the bedroom.

Ben had planned this morning for a week, ever since his wife of just a year had reacted so wonderfully to his fantasy story. He had gathered things from every source he could and now he just had to hope that Amy would go along with the game.

"Good morning, Mrs. Smith," Ben said. He was dressed in a light green scrub top and green scrub pants. Briefly, Amy wondered where he had gotten them. "If you'll just step into the bathroom and put this on, opening in the front, we can get on with your examination." Ben handed her a paper gown just like those in the doctor's office.

Amazed and excited, Amy stepped into the bathroom, quickly removed her clothes, and put the gown on. The feel of the scratchy paper against her skin was wonderfully arousing. Barefoot, she walked back into the bedroom.

"That's fine, Mrs. Smith," Ben said. "Now, if you'll just lie down here, we can begin." He pointed to the bed that he had covered with a plastic sheet and a layer of white paper.

Amy stretched out on the bed, waiting to see what would come next.

"Now, we'll begin with your eyes, nose, ears, and mouth." Ben used a wooden tongue depressor and a penlight to examine her. He even put an old-fashioned glass thermometer under her tongue, left it for two minutes, then removed it.

"That's fine. You seem healthy enough. Now for

your breasts." With a look of complete detachment on his face, Ben kneaded Amy's full breasts and tugged at her nipples. "They seem fine, my dear," he said, his voice very professional. "Now, we'll get you positioned for the rest of the exam." Ben spread Amy's knees wide, lifted two large pillows from the floor next to the bed, and put one under each knee. Amy's flesh was now wide open for the doctor's exam.

"First, I need gloves." Slowly, as his wife watched fascinated, Ben pulled on a pair of latex gloves. The plastic smell made Amy remember real doctor's office visits. Ben then brandished a bottle of rubbing alcohol and several cotton balls. As he soaked the cotton, he said, "I must sterilize the area." The smell was overpowering. It became hard to remember that this was her husband.

Fleetingly, Amy hoped that Ben knew that alcohol on her vaginal tissues would sting, but she needn't have worried. He rubbed the cold liquid on the insides of her thighs until she was "ready" for the exam.

He put the alcohol away and took out a tube of K-Y jelly. He squeezed a substantial amount into his hand and lubricated his fingers well. "Now for the exam."

With one hand, he pressed down on her lower belly as he inserted first one, then two, then three fingers of the other in her vagina. Then he slowly, sensually explored every crevice. He rubbed and stroked and probed, never moving the restraining hand on her lower belly.

As Amy started to move around, he said, his voice low and uninflected, "The doctor's almost through with this part. You must hold still." She tried to keep her body quiet as he probed and thrust and invaded her body. "That's a good girl," he said. "Now for the last part." Slowly, his slippery fingers worked backward until they were massaging the tissues surrounding her anus.

"Oh no, you don't have to do that." They had never tried anal sex and Amy wasn't sure it was decent. Ben had always wanted to explore his wife's body fully, so he took the choice away from her.

"Your exam isn't finished yet, dear," he said. "I just have to check out one more thing." Slowly, he pressed one finger against her anal opening. As he increased the pressure, he was surprised at how easily his latex-covered finger penetrated. Slowly, an inch at a time, he insinuated his finger into his wife's ass. He wanted to tell her how exciting this was, how soft and smooth she felt, but he didn't dare for fear of breaking the spell.

"Just a few more moments and the exam will be complete." Ben removed the restraining hand from his wife's belly and inserted two fingers into her sopping cunt. As he probed both openings, he felt her muscles tense. Suddenly, he wasn't the doctor anymore. He was a man fucking both his wife's orifices, making her come. "Come for me, baby. Do it."

"It's so good," she screamed. "Yes, *yes*."

He felt her orgasm, felt the waves of muscular contractions with both hands. It was amazing and fabulous. He kept moving inside of her until he felt her completely relax. Then he pulled off his gloves, removed the pillows from under her knees, and stretched out beside her on the bed.

"That was fantastic," she purred as she wrapped her arms around Ben. "I never imagined that it would be so exciting."

"You mean anal sex?"

"Ummm." She couldn't talk about it yet, but she knew she would learn. They had just discovered a new way to make love. "But what about you? You're still fully dressed."

"You just relax for a while and don't worry about the doctor. I have no more patients, so we have all day."

And lest you think that the idea of using all five senses to enhance a sexual experience is new, here is a story about a man using the same techniques several hundred years ago.

THE DUKE'S STORY

As the sun set and Duke John rode across the familiar fields near the castle, he found that he was looking forward to seeing his pretty young wife again. Wife: He let the word echo around in his mind. In some ways it was hard to accept the fact that he was indeed married. After all, he had only met Lady Kathryn a week before the wedding. After a less-than-spectacular wedding night, the duke had been forced by his duty to the king to leave for almost six weeks.

Lady Kathryn, he found that he had really missed her while he had been gone fighting a silly border skirmish. She was tiny, barely coming up to his chin, and more than passably pretty, with long chestnut hair, an oval face, and ivory skin. And she was interesting to talk to, in spite of the fact that she had spent most of her eighteen years with the holy sisters. But she was woefully ignorant in the ways of love, ways that Duke John had perfected over years of experience.

That first night together had proven difficult for his wife, the duke knew, but tonight he would make it up to her—and to himself. "There's a sensual and exciting woman under all that ignorance," he said aloud. "And, if I do things just right, I'm bound to free that fiery spirit." He smiled to himself. Yes, he thought, I'm looking forward to tonight.

As the large group approached the lowered drawbridge of the duke's castle, the group separated, most of the men continuing toward their own welcomes. Surrounded by only a few retainers, the duke rode into the main castle courtyard and saw Lady Kathryn waiting for him on the top step of the main building. When he caught her eye, he smiled at her. As she demurely lowered her eyes, he saw a glimpse of the smile that crossed her lovely features.

"Men," the duke said loudly, "it's late and I know all of you have places you wish to be. Tomorrow we will have a lavish feast to celebrate our victory, but for tonight, I bid you good evening."

With knowing looks at Lady Kathryn, a cheer went up from the assembled men. The duke dismounted and turned his horse over to a groom. He bounded up the steps and approached his wife. "Good evening, wife," he said. "I find I'm glad to be home and to see you looking so well."

Lady Kathryn slowly raised her eyes and looked at her handsome new husband. "I'm glad to see you too, my lord."

"I have some things to look to in the kitchen," the duke said, "but I'll join you upstairs in just a few minutes." He glanced at his wife and saw a blush redden her face. Then he turned and strode toward the kitchen.

Minutes later, Duke John opened the door to the room he now shared with his wife and walked inside. A fire blazed in the fireplace and rays of the setting sun glinted off the long curtain of Kathryn's hair. My wife is truly lovely, the Duke thought as he looked at her sitting demurely on the window seat, her feet drawn up under her and her hands clasped tightly in her lap.

The duke crossed the room and placed a light kiss on the top of Kathryn's head. "Don't be afraid, my dear," he whispered, his warm hands on her shoulders. "It won't be like our wedding night. I promise you that you will enjoy the evening and that I won't do anything that you aren't ready for. Do you understand what I'm saying?"

Nervously, she nodded. "Yes, my lord. I understand."

"First," the duke said, "you have to stop calling me my lord. My name is John. I'd like to hear you say my name." All he heard was an inaudible whisper. "Please, Kathryn. Say my name. Call me John."

"Yes, John, " she said. He smiled. His name sounded so sweet on her lips.

John backed away from his wife as a loud knock sounded at the door. "Enter," the duke called.

In walked three members of the kitchen staff, each with a silver tray. The duke motioned to a table near the fireplace and the three women put the trays down. "You can have the tub brought in a half an hour," he said.

As the three left, the duke held out his hand to Kathryn. "Come, Kathryn, and share my first meal back with me. I've ordered some wonderful delicacies for us to enjoy."

"I'm not hungry," Kathryn said, now almost huddled in the corner of the window seat.

"Darling," the duke said, "you'll have to learn to trust me. I won't hurt you, I promise. If I do anything that makes you unhappy or causes you pain, you have only to tell me and I'll stop immediately." He sat in one of the two chairs at the table. "Please, at least sit with me and share some wine."

Slowly, Kathryn uncurled her legs, rose, and hesitantly crossed the room. As she settled herself in the second chair, the duke said, "That's a good girl. Now, would you like some of the delicious food that cook has prepared?"

"No, thank you, my lord."

"John. You promised to call me John."

"No, thank you, John," she said.

The duke lifted the heavy silver wine carafe and

poured a large glass for Kathryn and one for himself. "You'll find that this wine is far superior to the poor, raw wine you got from the holy sisters. Try some."

Kathryn extended her hand and wrapped her slender fingers around the stem of the glass. Slowly, she lifted the delicate goblet to her lips and took a sip. She had never liked the rough red liquid that the sisters had given her at communion, nor had she enjoyed the watered brew they all drank at meals. This, however, tasted like nothing she had ever had at the convent. It was smooth and warm and tasted of fresh grapes and of rich brown earth. She looked at her husband and smiled. "It's very good."

"Wonderful. I'm glad you approve. Now, a toast to my successful mission and to the future gratitude of the king." They drank together.

As the meal progressed, the duke was pleased to see that his wife finally ate some of the roasted fowl and a piece of the fresh crusty bread. Several times at moments when Kathryn was occupied with her food, the duke refilled her wineglass.

"That was a lovely meal," Kathryn said, sitting back in her chair and sighing. The duke smiled as he realized that she was now talking on her own, not merely responding to his questions.

Another loud knock sounded at the door. "Enter," the duke said. The same three women entered and removed the remains of the meal while a group of men came in. Two carried a large wooden tub; the rest had buckets of steaming water. "Set that in front of the fire," the duke said, pointing to the huge bathing tub. Efficiently, the men set it up and filled it with the heated water. When the preparations were complete, the men withdrew, closing the large oaken door behind them.

"Now, my dear," the duke said, "I'm in need of a bath. I've been on the road for a week, hurrying home to you. We had little time for bathing."

"I'll attend to some things in my sitting room and come back when you're done," Kathryn said.

"Certainly not," the duke said. "You'll stay here and talk with me. I've been too long without you."

As the duke rose and began to remove his clothes, Kathryn nervously lowered her eyes and quickly turned her back. That's all right, the duke thought. Everything in its own good time.

Naked, Duke John climbed into the tub and settled back into the hot water. "This feels as wonderful as I knew it would." He sighed. "I've dreamt about a hot bath. And, my darling, I've also dreamt about the feel of your beautiful body. In the last few days, knowing I was so close to you, I've thought about touching your lips and perfect breasts often."

"My l-l-lord," Kathryn stammered, "you shouldn't speak like that."

"And why not? It was dark when we bedded on our wedding night and I was denied the sight of your skin. But still I know well how beautiful your body is. My lips touched your sweet mouth as I kissed you. My hands felt your tantalizing breasts with their small hard nipples as I caressed you. As my belly settled against yours, I brushed your smooth skin. And as I entered you—"

"Please, my lord, you shouldn't—"

"I should and I will. I will tell you how you look and how you taste and how you feel. If it makes you uncomfortable, then be silent for now. But I know that soon, you will feel differently. Soon you will not only be eager for my words but you will be telling me how good I feel. Soon you will be moaning and purring as I love you."

The duke turned and saw only his wife's back. Her back was tense and her shoulders were tightly set. He also heard her rapid breathing and could see her tremble. He knew that he was exciting her despite all her reservations. "All right," he said, laughing softly. "I will be still for now since I see how my talk upsets you. But, in return, I need for you to scrub my back. I'm thick with the dirt of the road and the smell of battle."

"My lord?"

"John. You promised."

"John, then. You want me to bathe you?"

"I want you to assist your husband. I need you to take a cloth and some soap and wash my back." When he sensed her continued hesitation, he added, "Is it so much to ask after so many weeks of battle?"

"It is not too much to ask," she admitted.

The duke heard the rustle of his wife's gown as she slowly turned and walked toward the tub. "Where is the cloth?" she asked softly.

"It is here in my hand, but you can't do anything in that long-sleeved gown. You'll be soaking wet in no time. Why don't you remove the gown so it won't get ruined?" When she did not immediately respond, he continued. "I won't bite you. I just need the help of my wife to wash where I can't reach."

Kathryn sighed, then began to remove her gown. When she was wearing only her chemise and pantalets, she walked up behind her husband. "May I have the cloth?"

The duke carefully avoided turning to look at his beautiful wife. He didn't want to frighten her or to increase his own excitement. He reached over his shoulder and handed her a piece of sweet-smelling soap and a cloth. Then he leaned forward to afford his wife free access to his back. As she washed him, the duke clenched his teeth and tried to calm his mounting desire.

After a few moments of enjoying his wife's stroking of his back, and with calculated suddenness, the duke leaned back. The abrupt movement had two immediate results. First, a large splash of water soaked the front of his wife's chemise; second, her right hand became trapped behind him. "I'm sorry," he said quickly. "I've gotten you wet. Let me help you."

Without freeing Kathryn's hand, Duke John reached for a towel, turned, and began to slowly rub the cloth over his wife's chest. He felt her try to pull back but he kept her hand imprisoned. "Don't run away, my love," he said as he sensuously stroked the towel over her breasts. "Please don't run away."

He watched as the wine and his stroking had the desired effect. Gradually, he saw her shoulders relax and her eyes close. He held the towel away from her breasts and saw two small, hardened brown buds through the now-transparent material. He knew what he wanted and he knew he risked frightening his silent wife, but he couldn't resist her.

Still keeping her hand trapped between his hip and the side of the tub, he leaned toward the nubby crests and took one nipple between his lips. Momentarily, she tried to pull back, then he felt her relax.

"So sweet," he murmured as he moved his mouth to her other breast. He sucked her puckered nipple and was rewarded by the sound of a soft moan deep in Kathryn's chest. "Yes, darling, enjoy. Don't be afraid. Let me make it feel so good."

"But the holy sisters said it was evil."

"Do you think it's evil?" He pinched her nipple and swirled his fingers over her soft flesh. "God intended us to love and create new life. That's why all this feels so good. Be honest with me. Be honest with yourself. Do you really think it's evil?"

He looked into her face and saw a small smile. "No. I think not," she whispered.

"Oh, my darling. It's so wonderful. You're so wonderful."

The duke leaned forward and wrapped his arms around Kathryn. Slowly, he lifted her up and onto his lap in the tub. "Trust me to make it good for you," he said hoarsely. The tiny purring sounds she made in her throat were his answer.

Now he allowed his hands the freedom to explore his wife's body. He stroked her ribs and her sides. He let some still-warm water trickle through his fingers onto her shoulders. He wet, then licked her neck and her ears. Then he let his lips and tongue explore her mouth.

Gradually, Kathryn began to return his kiss. Tentatively, her tongue met his and the tips caressed, stroked, tasted. Neither noticed exactly when Kathryn's hands began to move over her husband's chest, returning caress for caress.

Now John needed to relieve his aching cock and to pleasure his wife, as well. He let his hands slide lower, slipping easily between his wife's wet thighs. As she curled in his arms, he looked down to watch his hands slide over her dark curls and gently rub the hardened button he found beneath. He could feel the slickness of her juices through her pantalets.

As he wondered whether to rip the thin material, he felt Kathryn lift her hips to enable him to remove them, pressing her breast to his lips as she did so. Oh yes, she was a sensuous woman, wanting the pleasure that as yet she didn't fully understand but that he knew he could give her.

Kathryn settled back onto his lap in the water as he began rubbing and sliding his fingers between her legs.

"Oh, John," she whispered, "please."

"I know, darling. I know. Let me pleasure you."

"Oh yes."

He raised her hips and slid his body into position under hers. Then he slowly lowered her onto his pulsing cock. Inch by inch, he penetrated deep, never ceasing his stroking of her slick clit.

"John. Oh, John. Oh yes. Oh yes."

As he felt her begin to rhythmically squeeze her muscles around him, he could hold back no longer. With a roar, he came inside of her, pounding against her and splashing water over the side of the tub. As he spurted his seed, he felt her arch her back and heard her moan.

Slowly, their bodies calmed, their arms still wrapped around each other in the water. "Will it always be like that?" Kathryn asked.

John smiled. "Sometimes it will be even better."

Shyly, Kathryn looked up into her husband's eyes. "And sometimes will we do it in a dry bed?"

Their joined laughter could be heard all over the castle.

8

OVER AND OVER AGAIN

For our final stories, we will experience four of the five senses in a different way. We have spent all of our lives depending on our sense of sight. But, when deprived of our vision, other senses become heightened. In both of the stories in this chapter, couples make use of this fact. Like other stories in this book, the first story centers around a very special birthday present. Of course, if any of the ideas here appeal to you, you don't have to wait for a special occasion to try them.

MARY AND CLIFF'S STORY

It was Cliff's birthday. He and Mary, his wife of ten years, celebrated with their four children. There was a Carvel cake with candles and homemade gifts from each of the children. Cliff oohed and aahed over hand-crayoned birthday cards, a ceramic whatnot holder for his dresser, and a pencil holder made out of an old soup can for his desk. There was even an Aran Isle sweater from "Mommy."

Later, Cliff and Mary put the children to bed and went into their bedroom.

"I haven't given you the rest of my present yet," Mary said when they were at last alone.

"You mean there's more? That sweater was so beautiful. I'm amazed that you found time to shop."

"I hunted for the sweater, but this gift required no shopping." She handed Cliff an envelope.

Cliff opened the envelope and pulled out two cards. The first was from his in-laws. "Happy Birthday, Cliff," it said. "This is a gift certificate for a night without the children. We will pick them up late next Saturday afternoon and return them Sunday afternoon."

"Wow," Cliff said. "What a great gift, but I think they're out of their minds. Did you put them up to this?"

"I mentioned it to my folks and they quickly volunteered. I don't know where they'll find the time or the energy, but they seem willing to try."

"They're nuts, but wonderful. I love our four kids a lot, but they sure are a handful. Oh God, this means that for the first time in eight years, we can sleep on Sunday morning."

"Read the other card," Mary said, her voice low.

Cliff opened the second card, which said, "This entitles you to an evening with a woman who will do *whatever* you wish to please you. Please make maximum use of her."

"I want to make a fantasy of yours come true," Mary said. "I will follow any instructions, do anything." Then she smiled. "I rehearsed that speech all day," she said. "And I mean every word of it."

Cliff studied his wife's face. She really was serious.

"I need you to trust me," she continued, "to confide in me and either plan something totally unusual or tell me what you'd like to do. I want you to let go and create the most sensational night you've ever had."

All week, Cliff thought about what Mary had said. When they were first married, their sex life was terrific. Since the birth of the children, however, they had fallen into a routine that was barely satisfying, he had to admit. Usually, they were both too tired to spend much time playing. Most of their encounters were quickies.

Now Mary wanted to give him a night of pleasure like they had had before, maybe better.

By Friday afternoon, he had made his decision. He called his wife and told her that he would make all the arrangements for Saturday. She just had to go along with anything he wanted. Without hesitation, she agreed.

Saturday afternoon, Cliff made reservations at the small Chinese restaurant they had frequented before they were married. Then they packed the children off to their grandparents and treated themselves to a long, leisurely dinner.

Although she enjoyed the meal, Mary was a bit on

edge, curious to know exactly what Cliff had planned for later. She knew he had thought of something by the way he kept smiling and winking at her. She didn't ask, however, preferring to savor the anticipation.

When they arrived home, Cliff said, "I'll lock up the house. You go upstairs and put on some old clothes, ones you don't want back. I want everything disposable, down to your undies."

Mary was puzzled. Old clothes? What on earth did Cliff have in mind? She searched through her things and found and put on a pair of old panties. Since she had no bras she wanted to part with, she put on a much-painted-on sweatshirt over her bare skin. She quickly explored her closet and found a pair of sweatpants that had gotten too baggy for her to wear outside.

Donning a pair of stained socks, she called, "I'm ready."

Cliff mounted the stairs and entered the bedroom. "Very good," he said. "That's exactly what I wanted. Now," he said, motioning toward the bed, "lie down, faceup."

As Mary did as she was told, she noticed some old clothesline in Cliff's hand. She trembled in anticipation. Before the children, they had occasionally played at tying each other up. Mary found it very exciting.

"I see you've noticed what I have in my hand," Cliff said. "You said I could have anything I wanted and I know exactly what I want. Want to change your mind?"

"Not in the least," Mary said, her arms and legs

spread on the bed. "Remember our 'out word'? It was *mustard*."

"Right. If you say *mustard*, I'll stop whatever I'm doing."

Mary nodded as Cliff took her right wrist and carefully tied one piece of rope around it. Then he tied the other end to the headboard of the bed. Mary tested the rope and was pleased. He had remembered how he used to tie her up, not tightly enough to make marks but tightly enough that she couldn't get free.

While Mary pulled at her right wrist, Cliff tied her left one and both of her ankles. She was tied spread-eagled to the bed, still fully clothed.

"What are you going to do now?" she asked.

"Whatever I like, it seems."

While Mary watched, Cliff got a large cotton scarf and tied it loosely but securely across Mary's mouth. "Now," Cliff said, "just so I'm sure, say *mustard*."

The word came out "Uhhh uhhh," but Cliff and Mary understood. She could still end the game anytime she needed to.

"Now," Cliff said, "I need your undivided attention." He took another cotton scarf and tied it over Mary's eyes. "Very nice," he said. "Now I have your full concentration on each thing I do."

Mary heard Cliff walk into the bedroom and return a moment later. She heard a snipping sound.

"What you hear is the big pair of scissors you keep in the bathroom." Cliff put the scissors near Mary's ear so she could hear the blades snap together. "You can't speak and you can't see, but you can hear everything I do."

He knelt down near Mary's hips and pulled at the crotch of her sweatpants. "I want nothing in the way of your cunt," he said. Carefully pulling the fabric away from her body, Cliff cut the crotch out of both her sweatpants and her underpants. He reached in through the hole and felt her juices. "You're all wet," he said in mock surprise. "You must be a bad little girl to find this so exciting." He tickled her wet folds. "Yes, a very bad girl."

Mary was flying, so helpless and so excited. She tried to move her body, but Cliff stilled her. "Not so fast, darling," he said. "This might take all night."

Mary heard Cliff leave the room and go downstairs. She was so excited that she couldn't wait for him to return.

"I'm back," he said, his singsong voice mimicking Jack Nicholson's voice from *The Shining*.

Mary heard a clunking sound that she couldn't identify.

"Wondering what I have?" Cliff asked. "I'll show you. No," he said, looking at his wife's blindfolded eyes, "I guess show is not quite the right word." He lifted an ice cube from the bowl he was holding and touched it to Mary's hot vagina.

She jumped and sounds of pleasure and surprise came from her cotton-covered mouth.

"I thought that would cool you down for a few minutes." He slowly inserted a small ice chip into her vagina. As it melted, cool water trickled down between her cheeks. Suddenly, she felt the warmth of his tongue licking up the wet drops. Without a word, he stopped, sat up, and picked up the scissors.

"Now I want to suck your tits." He cut two circles from the front of her shirt so her breasts and nipples were exposed. "No bra, how convenient." He took one nipple and rolled it between his fingers while he bent and sucked the other into his mouth.

Mary was in heaven. Part of her wanted him to fuck her so she could climax, but part of her didn't want him to stop what he was doing. Suddenly, she realized that it didn't matter what she wanted. He was going to do whatever he wanted. She didn't have to think. She surrendered to the pleasures.

"I think I want you naked," Cliff said. Slowly he cut up the sleeves of the shirt, then he cut the shirt up the front. As he exposed various parts of Mary, he stopped to kiss and suck whenever he wished.

He moved to her feet and was about to cut the legs of her sweatpants when he stopped and reconsidered. "I think I'll leave these on," he said. "It would be kinky to fuck you through the noncrotch of your pants."

Quickly, he undressed and stretched his body over Mary's. His engorged penis stroked her vagina, wet with the last drops of melting ice with her juices. "Parts of your flesh are still cold," he said. "It's very erotic." He picked up another piece of ice and placed it against her folds, holding it in place and rubbing it around with his cock. "Very erotic."

Mary felt rivulets of melting ice trickle between her legs. She couldn't keep her hips still and moved them as much as her ropes would permit. She wanted, she needed...

He got up and again rubbed the ice cube over her hot, wet skin. Then he dropped the cube and stretched out over Mary's body. "This is wonderful. The combination of the heat of you and the cold of the melted ice water feel great." Slowly, with her sweatpants still in place, his cock reached her opening. With no effort, he slipped inside. "So good," he murmured. "You feel so good."

Slowly he withdrew, then pushed inside again. As he explored her body with his cock, he found cool and warm places deep inside her. Then he pulled out and pressed his cock into every fold of her.

Then he was inside, unable to stop moving. Much as he wanted this evening to last, he wanted them both to reach orgasm more. His hips slammed his cock inside of her and it took very little time before they both climaxed.

Later, Cliff untied Mary's ropes from the bed but left them tied around her wrists. "That's so we can save time in the morning," he whispered into her ear.

My friend Ed wrote this last story, a fantasy that you can act out if you wish. Over the years, Ed spent time with encounter groups and was involved in many sensual but nonsexual experiences. This story has grown out of those experiences. Two important things should be mentioned. First, the things that Mitch and Sonia do can be recreated in the bedroom by two consenting adults anytime. Although there is an element of menace in this story, menace in your sex games must be imaginary. Never should one party be *forced* to do anything. I don't think our hero was forced to do much after he relaxed and accepted the situation.

The second thing you may notice is that sensual and sexual are not necessarily the same thing. At first, what happens to Mitch is sensual, not erotic. Sonia starts out to instruct him in the uses of his senses of touch, smell, and taste. Only when she ventures into the sexual do the feelings change.

MITCH'S STORY

Although it had probably only been a few hours, it seemed like weeks since Mitch had been brought to this darkened room by agents of The Movement. He recalled that he had been about to go into the all-night grocery to buy a six-pack of beer when a car had pulled up next to him and a young woman had opened the window and had politely asked directions to Plainville. As he had approached the car, he had been grabbed from behind and thrown into the back. He remembered being held by strong hands, something soft being held over his nose and mouth and the sickly sweet smell of ether. Then nothing.

He had been in this small, dark, windowless room since he had awakened. For some reason he couldn't understand, he wasn't afraid. He wasn't tied up and, although he was naked, he was not uncomfortable in the warmly heated air. He had explored the space using his sense of touch, but the room was bare—not a single piece of furniture—only the soft wall-to-wall carpet on which he sat. Once, a few hours ago, someone had come in and turned on the light. He had quickly looked around the room for some clue as to where he was, but he saw nothing useful. He hadn't even gotten a good look at the man who had given him water and then blindfolded him and taken him out to use the bathroom. He had been given no food. He could not remember ever having been so hungry.

Suddenly, the door opened. As Mitch squinted against the bright light of the doorway, he could see the silhouette of a woman entering the room. As she closed the door behind her, she told him in a soft but firm voice that he would be fed now, but only if he did exactly as he was told. If he resisted, attempted to escape or disobeyed any order, he would not be fed for another six hours, at which time he would be given the same choice. Hungry and feeling helpless, Mitch quickly agreed. The woman ordered him to kneel on the floor facing the wall. With little choice, Mitch did as he was told. He heard the woman come up behind him and then felt soft material being wound across his eyes and behind his head. For Mitch, it was now as dark as it had been in the room with the door closed.

Mitch wanted to reach up and remove the blindfold, but something told him to bide his time. He wanted to find out what was going on before he tried to escape. After the blindfold was in place, Mitch was told to turn and sit on the floor.

"My name is Sonia," the woman said. "I am a lieutenant in The Movement."

Her voice was not unpleasant and it was impossible for Mitch to tell whether she was old or young. From her silhouette in the doorway, he had been able to tell only that she was of medium height.

"You have been chosen to become a member of our group," she continued.

"But I don't—" Mitch started to say.

"Be quiet!" Sonia snapped, her voice suddenly hard. "What you want or don't want no longer has any significance. We've been watching you and we know that you will be perfect for what we have in mind."

Mitch was mystified. What did she know about him? What were they planning and what was all this darkened room and blindfold business?

"You have been selected to become a member of our movement," Sonia continued. "You will be taught everything you need to know to serve the cause as time passes."

As Sonia spoke, Mitch realized that, be it conviction or fanaticism, she would stop at nothing to further The Movement, whatever that was. He knew that he had to go along with whatever she wanted.

"Your training will begin now and I have been assigned to teach you two lessons. First, you must learn self-discipline. Second, you must be able to rely on all of your senses, not only your vision but also taste, smell, touch—like the animals. I know that you are hungry, and I am going to feed you. But you will not be permitted to satisfy your hunger quickly. As I feed you, you will be told exactly how to eat. If you disobey any order, the food will be removed for six hours.

"And also," Sonia added softly, "keep in mind that before you can become a member of our movement, you must learn to please your superiors in every way."

As she spoke the last words, Mitch felt her cool hand slide between his legs and momentarily press against his cock and balls. Then her hand was gone.

In a soft voice, Sonia said, "I will press various items of food against your lips for you to feel and smell. Then, when I tell you to, you will open your mouth just wide enough for me to put the morsel into your mouth. You will then wait for further orders. If you make any attempt to bite or chew...well, I needn't repeat what will happen."

Mitch heard a rustling sound as Sonia chose an item to feed him. Then he felt something cool against his lips. Hungrily, he opened his mouth.

"I will tell you when to part your lips." Sonia pressed her fingers under his chin, forcing Mitch to close his mouth. "First, I want you to feel and smell."

Mitch felt the cool, smooth object rubbed over his lips. There was a slightly pungent aroma. Although he was hungry, he was wise enough to keep his lips together.

"Now you may part your lips, just a bit."

Mitch opened his mouth.

"Much too wide," Sonia scolded.

Mitch closed his mouth until his lips were barely separated.

"That's a lot better. You learn quickly."

Mitch felt a small, round, smooth object pressed into his mouth, then Sonia's fingertips on his lips. The urge to chew and swallow the food was almost overwhelming.

As if reading his mind, Sonia whispered, her lips close to his hear, "Don't you dare."

Mitch sat still, the object cool on his tongue.

"I have fed you a grape," Sonia said. "Roll it around in your mouth. I know you're hungry and want to swallow it, but I want you to feel it. Feel its roundness. Press against it with your tongue and feel its elasticity. You will do what I want you to do, not what you want to do."

Mitch did as he was told, realizing that if he did not, he was going to become much hungrier in the next six hours.

"Now bite it in half, but don't chew it. Taste the inside with your tongue."

As he did so, Mitch felt dizzy with hunger. But he also realized that never had a grape tasted as sweet before. After what seemed like an eternity of feeling and tasting, Mitch was allowed to chew very slowly and swallow the grape.

Over the next hour, the process was repeated with various small bits of food: soft Camembert, pieces of hard-boiled egg, freshly baked warm bread, lettuce, strawberries.

"You must be thirsty after all that food," Sonia said. Then Mitch heard her breath close to his face and felt her lips against his mouth. Her mouth was closed but her lips pressed insistently against his. As he started to open his mouth, he felt a warm, fragrant liquid seep into his mouth. Sonia reached behind him and pressed her hand against the back of his head, forcing his mouth against her slowly parting lips.

It was wine, Mitch realized. It flowed and swirled between them. A trickle flowed out of the corner of their joined mouths and dripped on Mitch's naked thigh. It felt like the warm wax drippings of a burning candle. Their tongues touched, caressed, and tasted each other and the pungent wine. At first, Mitch did not swallow the wine out of fear, then he felt Sonia's lips soften and he swallowed the precious liquid.

Mitch felt Sonia pull away, then again press her lips against his. He swallowed another mouthful. Soon the sensations of the wine and Sonia's mouth and tongue made Mitch forget his hunger for food and stimulated a new hunger.

Sonia's voice had grown much gentler now. She told Mitch that she was now going to feed him in a different way. He would be allowed to swallow when he wished but would not be given anything more until he had finished every drop of what had been served to him.

Mitch felt Sonia move away from him and he was aware of rustling sounds. Then he sensed her draw near. Unlike the previous times she had fed him, when he had heard a rustle and felt the sleeve of a garment touch his skin as she approached, this time he heard nothing but her breathing. He was aware of her nearness even though he couldn't see her. He smelled the clean, slightly pungent scent of her body, heard her breathing, and felt an approaching warmth.

Mitch felt the light touch of something hard and warm against his lips. As he opened his mouth to receive the morsel, Sonia grasped the hair on the back of his head and pulled. Then Mitch felt what he now realized was her nipple and breast force itself into his mouth.

"Now suck," she ordered.

He sucked her swollen nipple and hot breast and the sweet taste of maple syrup filled his mouth.

"Remember what I told you. Every drop," she reminded him.

He licked and sucked, his tongue covering every inch of her heated flesh. He reached up to hold her, but she pushed his hands back down to his sides.

When she was satisfied that he had finished every drop of the syrup, Sonia fed him the other breast, likewise covered with maple syrup.

By now, Mitch's hunger for food had been entirely replaced by sexual hunger. Although he was allowed to suck her tit, Mitch was not allowed to touch Sonia in any way, nor did she touch him other than an occasional exploration between his legs to evaluate his state of hunger.

After Mitch had finished sucking all of the syrup off of Sonia's breasts, she again moved away. When she returned, she ordered him to lie on his back. She told him that he had to be taught to improve his sucking and licking skills.

He became aware of Sonia positioning her body above his face. Then, as she lowered herself, he felt her body heat and her coarse pubic hair against his mouth and smelled her strong, sweet, pungent vaginal aroma. He felt her fingers reach between her legs to separate her labia so that he could begin to suck and lick her hidden hot flesh. This time, there was no syrup, just the sweet flavor of her own juices.

"Ohhh, that's very good Mitch," Sonia said breathlessly as he licked, alternately raising herself almost out of reach of Mitch's mouth, then lowering her hips and grinding her wet flesh against his mouth and nose. "But you need to be shown how to do it even better."

Sonia was facing Mitch's feet as he sucked, licked, and began to penetrate Sonia's cunt with his tongue. She leaned forward, and Mitch heard a jar opening and a slurping sound. Then he felt Sonia's hands covering his penis and balls with a warm, sticky substance. Momentarily, he stopped sucking. Suddenly, he felt Sonia's hands tighten on his balls and he cried out in pain.

"Did I give you permission to stop sucking my cunt?" she asked, as if talking to a naughty child.

"No."

"Well then, I trust you will not make it necessary for me to punish you again," she said, caressing Mitch's aching testicles.

Mitch resumed his sucking, taking Sonia's clitoris in his mouth and teasing it with his tongue.

As Sonia continued to coat Mitch's cock and balls with the sticky liquid, she said, "Now, as I suck, you suck. As you feel my rhythm, you adjust your rhythm."

Mitch felt the flick of her tongue on his stiff cock.

Then she waited. Mitch flicked the tip of his tongue over her clit.

"That's very good," she said. "You learn very quickly." She smoothed her tongue the length of him and he slid his tongue along her slit. "Ummm," she purred. "Very good indeed. But don't you dare come until I give you permission. Do you understand?"

"I understand," Mitch said. Then he resumed licking her hot flesh.

As she sucked his cock, he sucked her cunt. When she licked quickly, his tongue moved in the same rhythm. When she wrapped her mouth around him and took the length of his cock into her mouth, he sucked her clitoris into his mouth. By varying her sucking, she instructed him as to how she wanted to be sucked.

Soon the feel of Mitch's tongue between her legs became overwhelming. As she felt the spasms of orgasm wash over her body, she reflexively wrapped her hands tightly around Mitch's penis, her hand movements now pumping his cock.

As Mitch felt Sonia's hips buck and grind against his mouth and felt her hands relentlessly pumping his swollen cock, he realized that he could not hold out much longer. He knew that he was not allowed to come without permission, but his body was beginning to lose control.

Then Mitch felt Sonia's spasms begin to lessen as her orgasm subsided. Her grip on his cock loosened and the movement of her hips stopped. He felt her hands leave his body. Relieved, he began to feel himself in control again, although he was hotter than he had ever been in his life. As soon as I'm alone, I'll relieve myself, he thought.

Suddenly, he felt Sonia's cold, slippery finger pressing against his asshole and her other hand wrap itself tightly around his cock. With one swift thrust, Sonia slid her finger deep into Mitch's ass while her other hand tightly held his cock. Then, sliding her finger in and out of his ass, she bent over and took his cock deep into her mouth, sucking as hard as she could.

As soon as she began to feel the first throbs of his orgasm, she took his penis out of her mouth, wrapped her slippery hand around his cock, and, still fucking his ass with her finger, pumped his cock until she could watch his semen spurting into the air.

As his ragged breathing slowed, Mitch felt Sonia move away and heard the rustle of her clothing as she dressed. Then he heard her approach him and felt the blindfold being removed. The room was dark. Then he heard her soft but firm voice.

"You were not given permission to come, but you came anyway, Mitch. It's clear that you need many more lessons in how to be obedient. I'll be back later for another lesson. You may not believe it now, but someday you, too, will be teaching new recruits how to serve our cause."

The door opened and Mitch watched the silhouette of Sonia leave the room. The door closed and it was dark again. Mitch was still hungry.

IN CONCLUSION

I hope that while reading this book, you had many ideas and are even now thinking about ways to spice up your love life. Whether you've decided to change your perfume, wear leather, or stroke the inside of your partner's thigh with ice, I hope you will enjoy expanding the range of your fantasies and activities and that you and your partner share many wonderful times in the future.

Keep an open mind at all times and include all your senses in your lovemaking. The next time you shop, wander the supermarket and think about what can be done with the taste of salad dressing or the feel of a cucumber. Walk through a department store and imagine the sight of a naked body wrapped only in a tiny new towel or brief robe. Don't overlook the smell of incense or the sound of different music. Explore.

Keep varying your sexual routine. If you have more ideas than you can fit into one evening, store up scenarios for other nights. Just planning can keep the juices flowing.

Don't hesitate to come back to this book in a month or two and search for new ideas. Read different sections aloud. Make up new stories. Put them into action.

Just remember that the basis of creativity is communication. Share your ideas, your fears, your secrets and you can increase your pleasures a hundredfold. But most important, have fun.

Dear Reader,

I hope you've enjoyed If It Feels Good... *and that you've found a few of my ideas pleasurable. By now, you've learned to use your sexual senses in new ways and maybe you've expanded and tried some things that are not mentioned in this book. Since Ed and I are always anxious for new experiences, please write and share any ideas with us.*

Write to Joan Elizabeth Lloyd, c/o Warner Books, Inc., Time & Life Building, 1271 Avenue of the Americas, New York, NY 10020.

Thanks for any suggestions.